Will This Place Ever Feel Like Home?

SIMPLE ADVICE FOR

SETTLING IN AFTER

YOUR MOVE

LESLIE LEVINE

Real Estate
Education Company®
a division of Dearborn Financial Publishing, Inc.

This publication is designed to provide accurate and authoritative information in regard to the subject matter covered. It is sold with the understanding that the publisher is not engaged in rendering legal, accounting, or other professional service. If legal advice or other expert assistance is required, the services of a competent professional person should be sought.

Acquisitions Editor: Danielle Egan-Miller
Managing Editor: Jack Kiburz
Interior Design: Elizandro Carrington
Cover Design: Design Alliance, Inc.
Typesetting: Elizabeth Pitts

The author is grateful to the following who have graciously granted permission to reprint:

- Bruce Henderson "The Wheels Roll" lyrics printed by kind permission. Lyrics Copyright 1997 Senator Dog Music (ASCAP).
- Child Care Aware
- National Family Caregivers Association, *Principles of Caregiver Self Advocacy*
- From *Home Sweeter Home* © 1996 by Jann Mitchell, Beyond Words Publishing, Inc. 800-284-9673

Published by Real Estate Education Company®,
a division of Dearborn Financial Publishing, Inc.®

Printed in the United States of America

98 99 00 10 9 8 7 6 5 4 3 2 1

Library of Congress Cataloging-in-Publication Data

Levine, Leslie
    Will this place ever feel like home? : simple advice for settling
in after your move / by Leslie Levine.
        p. cm.
    Includes bibliographical references and index.
    ISBN 0-7931-2870-6 (pbk.)
    1. Moving, Household.   I. Title.
TX307.L48   1998
648′.9−dc21   98-38605
                                                        CIP

Real Estate Education Company books are available at special quantity discounts to use as premiums and sales promotions, or for use in corporate training programs. For more information, please call the Special Sales Manager at 800-621-9621, ext. 4384, or write to Dearborn Financial Publishing, Inc., 155 N. Wacker Drive, Chicago, IL 60606-1719.

Advance Praise for
Will This Place Ever Feel Like Home?

❖ ❖ ❖ ❖ ❖ ❖ ❖ ❖ ❖ ❖ ❖ ❖ ❖ ❖ ❖ ❖ ❖

"Leslie Levine has thrown out a real lifesaver ring for men and women in the emotional turbulence of any move or relocation."

> –Vicki Lansky
> Author, *Practical Parenting Tips* and other parenting books
> Contributing Editor, *Family Circle* magazine

"Whether you're relocating for the first time or have been uprooted many times before, whether you're on your own or moving with your family, you'll find *Will This Place Ever Feel Like Home?* to be an indispensable guide to one of life's most difficult transitions. With topics ranging widely and wisely from home to school to workplace, this book is as up-to-date as the Internet and as time tested as the Welcome Wagon. Read this book for yourself, for your family, for the old friends you leave behind, and for the new ones you'll meet."

> –Dan Dubner, MD
> Author, *The Pediatrician's Best Baby Planner for the
> First Year of Life*

"Whether you're moving yourself, your aging parents, or your entire family, including the dog, *Will This Place Ever Feel Like Home?* should get packed along with your other valuables. It's a welcome all-in-one resource that not only helps with good-byes and moving on, but more importantly with hellos and moving in."

> –Jane Murphy
> Coauthor, *STAY TUNED! Raising Media Savvy Kids in the
> Age of the Channel-Surfing Couch Potato,* and Partner,
> Kidvidz, Inc.

"Leslie's practical 'been there, done that' advice for relocating families is a refreshing look at the many challenges faced by families who move to a new location. *Will This Place Ever Feel Like Home?* offers practical, sound advice for dealing with the very real issues of trailing spouses, 'dislocation,' challenges faced by children, and the overall process of assimilating into a new community. I would definitely recommend this book for transferees and relocation administrators alike."

> —Rod Reimann
> Senior Consultant, Runzheimer International

"In *Will This Place Ever Feel Like Home?* Leslie Levine has gone to the very essence of the human condition during the 'dislocation' process. Her research is solid and her prescription for settling in is meaningful, while offered with an understanding warmth. Families and individuals of every composition and description who face a move will find this work helpful and reassuring."

> —J. Stephen Mumma
> Senior Vice President, Marketing, *Atlas Van Lines*
> (Evansville, Indiana)

"Ms. Levine's book deals with a subject that is a major source of anxiety and emotional stress for today's labor force. And as increasingly larger numbers of those who relocate have working spouses and dependents, the problems become even more difficult. *Will This Place Ever Feel Like Home?* contains a wealth of practical advice that will help both employees who move and the companies that move them."

> —Charles S. Rogers
> Chairman, WFD (Work/Family Directions)

"I found *Will This Place Ever Feel Like Home?* to be insightful, educational, and filled with strategies to deal with the complexities of relocating. A true resource that provides assistance to anyone moving!"

> —Charlie Morris
> President, Northeast Region, Prudential Relocation

Dedication

For my father (1921–1997) who taught me the healing and restorative powers of a well-stocked toolbox.

Contents

Foreword

❖ ❖ ❖ ❖ ❖ ❖ ❖ ❖ ❖ ❖ ❖ ❖ ❖ ❖ ❖ ❖ ❖

It was April and I was 40. I'd taken three days to drive from the East Coast to the Midwest, accompanied by a computer, a photocopier, and three cats. At least the computer and the photocopier didn't yowl on every interstate between Connecticut and Kansas.

I had moved for the least inspirational of reasons: a relationship had not worked out, and I didn't trust my earning ability to sustain my daughter and myself in New York City. So we were coming home. Rachael stayed with friends so could I drive out first, meet the moving truck, and have a week to make the apartment really inviting.

I looked around the flat that I'd thought was "adorable" when the real estate agent showed us around the month before. This night, furnished only with office equipment and a litter box, the place looked as desolate as I felt. I surveyed the rooms, trying to come up with a positive thought, when I heard—what was it?— sawing, whirring, roaring, distinctly. The agent hadn't mentioned that the upstairs tenant in this duplex was a woodworker—a nighttime woodworker. My response was immediate and appropriate: I sat on a suitcase and cried.

That was eight years ago. I arranged a truce with the woodworker (who eventually moved). The furniture arrived and fit. Rachael flew out with her best friend Ashley and Ashley's mom, who encouraged us to put in a vegetable garden. We bought a used piano and adopted a homeless kitten. That little apartment on Bell Street in Kansas City became such a center of life and energy that it inspired me to write a book about home, *Shelter for the Spirit*. That's how Leslie Levine came to know me, and I became privileged to write the Foreword for *Will This Place Ever Feel Like Home?*

As I read Leslie's knowledgeable and empathetic guide to every aspect of relocating, I kept flashing back to that dismal April night in my empty apartment. If only I'd had Leslie Levine's keen insights and practical suggestions then!

Because our society is so mobile, we forget to our peril that *uprooting* is not just a euphemism for moving: it's what really happens. We're pulled up and taken away from what's familiar, from the sources of nourishment we've grown to depend on. We're stuck somewhere else, in alien soil, and expected to do just fine.

It's no wonder that on a psychologist's stress scale, moving falls between loss of a job and divorce. Compounding the anxiety, other stressors, such as a new job or a new marriage, often precipitate the move itself. This means that at the times when we most need that window seat in the guest bedroom or the big cottonwood tree in the backyard, we're somewhere else, trying to bond with different trees, different views, and—if we've moved a substantial distance—different people.

There are plenty of excellent books to help us through the challenges that accompany work, relationships, marriage, children, health, finances, and life's inevitable losses. To my knowledge, Leslie Levine is the first author to notice that moving is the curious blend of loss and gain that affects every other aspect of life. Whether the move is inspired by what feels like triumph or failure, every person who leaves one home for another needs information, understanding, and support. *Will This Place Ever Feel Like Home?* provides all three.

Like having a patient friend you can call at all hours and reverse the charges, *Will This Place Ever Feel Like Home?* is there to let you know that whatever you're feeling is normal under the circumstances. And, whatever specific problem you're facing has a solution—quite likely one given on the information-packed pages you're about to read.

Another lovely gift from Leslie Levine's book is that you don't have to dig to get the answers you're looking for. Good grief, you may have just packed 213 boxes, the last 27 of which say "Miscellaneous." There could never be a better time for clear, concise, and blessedly simple instructions on what to do next. Although reading this book cover-to-cover is pure delight, you can use Leslie's to-the-point bulleted lists and her "Taking Inventory" sections at the end of each chapter to deal with almost any crisis that comes up. When you're feeling weary and displaced, there's real comfort in having a compassionate mentor say, "Do this. It will make things better."

Believe me, it does. As I read *Will This Place Ever Feel Like Home?*, I was seven months past both moving and getting married. I figured it would take a couple of years to feel truly ensconced here, to get used to sharing space in an expanded family group, and to blend my personality with that of a house built when my grandmother was a girl. Reading this book cut my learning curve—and my comfort curve—decidedly short.

I took Leslie's suggestions for having "talismans," items of personal meaning, out, available, and abundant. I found in Leslie's words the voice of a kindred soul when it comes to buying locally and cultivating a network of "social support" through friendly grocery clerks and cheerful hairdressers. And, thanks to Chapter 3, "Relocating Spouses and Partners," my husband and I meet for a monthly lunch *and* we're committed to having a new—and *interesting*—couple over for dinner just as often.

Leslie astutely sees that creating a home isn't just getting the final box unpacked, it's a willingness to build a consciousness that supports every person in the household. This consciousness, this true feeling of home, can fill your house or apartment with graciousness, warmth, and peace.

The really remarkable thing is that this feeling doesn't have to stay at 1401 Cedar Street or wherever you've established it. You can take it with you. You can take the "homeyness" you built in the residence you're leaving and reinstall it in the new location. Add the counsel from Leslie, plus creativity and love from you, and one of these days, you'll walk in, stretch out on your bed, and think to yourself, "Gosh, it's good to be home."

—Victoria Moran, Author
of *Shelter for the Spirit:*
How to Create Your Own
Haven in a Hectic World

Author's Note

Over the course of a few years, I interviewed more than 120 people for this book. I spoke with people who've relocated as well as the professionals who are trained to facilitate these moves. I tried to incorporate in my sample a variety of cultural, economic, and geographic backgrounds. I also talked with a number of experts from varying disciplines. Everyone interviewed spoke openly and freely, though in some cases I was asked to protect and respect people's anonymity. To honor those requests, I have occasionally altered names and identifying details of certain people and places in the book.

If what you read in these pages inspires you to share your thoughts, please write to me at:

P.O. Box 2306
Northbrook, IL 60062
Or e-mail me at Leslie@housewarming.com

Preface

▦ ❖ ▦ ❖ ▦ ❖ ▦ ❖ ▦ ❖ ▦ ❖ ▦ ❖ ▦ ❖ ▦

She said how will you know when
you get to where you want to be
I said if I knew the answer there
might be a home for me

—Bruce Henderson, "The Wheels Roll"

Seven years ago, I joined the ranks of first-time movers. I had given up a good job to relocate to the Northeast for my husband's career. With my professional life in limbo, I was free to devote my time and energy to getting us and our 18-month-old daughter acclimated to our new surroundings. I threw myself into relocating with genuine enthusiasm. Yet once my husband began his new job and our utilities were up and running, the reality of relocating became painfully apparent. I felt like a "summer person" surrounded by year-round residents. I was an outsider.

To alleviate the alienation and loneliness, I sought resources that would help me adjust to my new city. Although the community offered a vast array of activities and points of interest, the literature I found on relocating was limited and terribly outdated. The books I did find generally devoted only a few pages to settling in; those that did blend moving and the adjustment that follows were scholarly studies. I wanted something more.

In the absence of finding a book on settling in, I searched for other relocated people, hoping to learn how they had successfully adjusted to their new homes and communities. People generously shared their wisdom and tips over coffee, in the child care center's parking lot, over fruits and vegetables in the grocery store, and during telephone conversations. It occurred to me then that people who relocate—for whatever reason—might benefit from this personal, homespun, and, in most cases, tried-and-true advice. Why not capture this information, consolidate it into a useful format, and share it with others?

I began asking people—movers and the professionals whose services they rely on—if such a collection of tips would be useful. Everyone responded with a resounding, "Yes! Absolutely!" My hope is that the personal and professional insights presented in *Will This Place Ever Feel Like Home?* will give you the means to complete your transition.

Oddly enough, as I complete the manuscript for this book, I am preparing to move again, this time to the Midwest. My plan is to say hello to its spirit and shake hands with its soul. I think I'm ready.

Acknowledgments

This book would be a mere shell without the contributions of and the collective leap of faith by so many people. I wish to thank Azriela Jaffe for her friendship, generosity, and steady encouragement; my enthusiastic and savvy editor and friend Danielle Egan-Miller for harnessing this shooting star and keeping it on course; and Sandy Beckwith and Alice Fixx for help in preparing my proposal.

For his interest and direction early on I thank Stedman Mays. I am also grateful to Elly Sidel who provided invaluable insight when the book was in its infancy.

To all the people who entrusted me with their memories, hopes, and dreams, I am immensely grateful and hope that I have accurately captured your sentiments. I also am indebted to those who shared their experiences but whose privacy I promised to protect; this book would not be the same without their rich and generous input.

I also relied upon the experience and wisdom of several industry experts. Appreciation goes to Diane MacPherson for her priceless insight and for always listening; Pete Packer for his support and steady flow of statistics; Steve Mumma for giving me the opportunity to share my work before an audience; George Bennett for his knowledge and kindness; Gail Curran for telling me about Dearborn; Jennifer Lugar for her time and perspective; and Larry Long of the U.S. Census Bureau for helping me decipher the demographics.

I also am tremendously grateful to Susan Ginsberg for her invaluable knowledge and constant encouragement. A special thank you goes to Victoria Moran for her kind words and for what her writing has taught me about the meaning of home. My nod to Sylvia Ackley whose "After the Boxes" workshop inspired me to think about writing this book. Thank you to Bill Thomas for scouting out the lyrics.

My deepest gratitude as well to the following for their keen and insightful input: Judith Holender Loeb, Amy Mirran, Gloria Bartholemew, Tim Weider, Deb Nicholas and her colleagues at Career Development Services, Jim Huth, Howard Mitchell, Mara Adelman, Susan Page, Ann Marie Mariarty, Sue Bender, Carolyn White, Larry Bennett, Richard Nelson Bolles, Sharon Richards, Jo Robinson, Scott Stanley, Maryann McCabe, Richard Grana, Morris Wessel, Matt Lopreiato, Lynn Halik, Sue Gager, Rosie Conley, Ro Logrippo, Elaine O'Neil, John Willis, Murray Kappelman, Vivian Katzenstein-Friedman, Rosalind Barnett, Mike McIntyre, Robin Hardman, Cheryl Kaiser, Brad Landsman, Steve Reiter, Neal Lenarsky, Jim Anderson, Ann Young, Fiona Wong, Ruth Davis, Laura Herring, Patricia Nealon, Cornelius Grove, Bill Fontana, Andy Fleming, and Jacque Schultz.

A big thank you to the wizards at www.profnet.com for helping me find just what I went looking for; Scott Forbes for coercing my computer to do the right thing; and Joie Harris, Judy Serck, Rick Leasure, Mary Robbins, Linda Baldwin, and Robert Galardi for helping me and my family get from here to there. For their help and support, I am grateful to the Pittsford New York Library, the babysitting services of the Jewish Community Center of Rochester, New York, St. John Fisher College Child Care, Sam Crawshaw, Joyce Paley, and various Allen Creek moms who covered for me during deadline crunches. For their generous support I thank Richard Arnold and Rabbi Alan Katz. Also, a special thank you to Allen Mendler who said, "Just do it." And so I did. For delivering my book to all points north, south, east, and west, I thank the Pittsford, New York, Post Office.

I have been enormously blessed by the talented team at Dearborn and am most grateful to Dani Cryssanthou, Julie Helmstetter, Sandy Holzbach, Lucy Jenkins, Eileen Johnson, Jack Kiburz, Christine Litavsky, Paul Mallon, Bobbye Middendorf, Elizabeth Pitts, Trey Thoelcke, and Cynthia Zigmund. Special thanks goes to Lynn Schneidhorst Olson for her excellent copyediting skills. Many thanks to Patti Danos, publicist extraordinaire.

Writing a book spirits you away from friends and family. Yet without their steady presence and sustenance, this book could never have been completed. For their inspiration, friendship, and unconditional support, I offer my deepest thanks to my personal editorial committee—those who, at a moment's notice, read, listened to, and offered their comments on my work-in-progress: Hope DeCederfelt, Christina Rossomando, Robin Weintraub LaBorwit, Pat DeLuca, Alice de Mauriac, Kathy Driscoll, Nancy Dhurjaty, Colleen Kaiser, Chrissy Larson, and Phyllis Wagner. My very special thanks goes to Pam Bernstein, Tris Downer, Jerry Flach, Betty Hancock, Susan Harf, Sharon Hoffmann, Martha Kirkley, Holli Levy, Jean Mumford, Lauren Nathan, Leslie Schwartz, Evy Severino, Mary Spurrier, and Sabra Wood for their friendship and for cheering me on at all the right moments.

For their steady support and love I wish to thank my mother, Elinor Zevin; my sister, Wendy Zevin, and my brother, Robert Zevin. Warm thanks as well to Helen and Jerry Levine and Sheri and Steve Levine.

My children, Esther and Philip, endured perhaps the greatest hardship during the research and writing of this book. From their deadline-driven mama I offer them my sense of awe, complete love, and very deepest thanks.

More than anyone, it is my husband Jonathan who gave me the time and space to dream and then later, the same so that I could, indeed, catch the dream; my most heartfelt appreciation to Jon in whose company my place will always feel like home.

Introduction

❖ ❖ ❖ ❖ ❖ ❖ ❖ ❖ ❖ ❖ ❖ ❖ ❖ ❖ ❖ ❖ ❖

"Home" is any four walls that enclose the right person.

—Helen Rowland, *Reflections of a Bachelor Girl*

Moving is about saying good-bye. The information in this book will help you say hello.

Americans move. Whether we're changing jobs, retiring, or just making a fresh start, we've turned relocating into a national pastime. According to the U.S. Census Bureau, an astounding 16 percent of the population moves every year. Indeed, the U.S. military is in the midst of discharging nearly a million personnel, many of whom will relocate to new communities.

Whether you have purchased a home or are renting someone else's property, *Will This Place Ever Feel Like Home?* will take you beyond the administrative tasks associated with moving, such as arranging for gas and electric service, establishing new bank accounts, and getting your cable TV hooked up. The book is written for people facing the colossal task of making a new home for themselves—one of life's most difficult challenges, indeed, one of life's most significant *changes.* Yet even in the midst of change, we can achieve control in some very fundamental ways. We can control our outlooks. We can control how far we're willing to go to get what we need and want.

Coupled with your own inner strength and the support systems in your life, *Will This Place Ever Feel Like Home?* will help you recreate home, make meaningful connections in your new community, and preserve your sense of self. I hope that what you find within these pages will assure you that you are not alone in your feelings of isolation, loss, and confusion.

Will This Place Ever Feel Like Home? will help you get a jump start on the adjustment process. This book features some personal accounts of people who have moved and successfully settled into their new locations. Also included are insights and advice from numerous professionals in relocation and related industries. I've also added lots of practical advice to help you navigate specific situations and emotions that are likely to surface after you've waved good-bye to the moving van and unpacked the last box.

Will This Place Ever Feel Like Home? is a source of ideas, practical solutions, and comfort. Use it as a guide for scouting out a new life. In each chapter you will find a number of ways to say hello and become acclimated to your new life. If you're a relocating spouse, for instance, you'll learn how to collaborate with your partner so that each of you can find fulfillment in your new lives. If you have children, you'll discover fun and whimsical ways to minimize the sense of loss that kids experience after moving from the familiar to the unknown.

Through several personal accounts, including my own, you will find that the broad range of feelings—from loss, sadness, and bewilderment to hope, excitement, and exhilaration—are universal and that the strategies, tactics, and tips that have worked for others can help you as well. You can read this book in a number of different ways. You may want to read it from start to finish or pick and choose among the chapters that seem to apply to your particular situation. Piece together your own strand of wisdom. Because while moving is in many ways a common occurrence, the truth is only *you* can make your place feel like home.

Chapter 1

Uprooting:
A Major Upheaval

To be rooted is perhaps the most important
and least recognized need of the human soul.
—Simone Weil, *The Need for Roots*

When I asked my friend Susan how she coped after moving from her home state to another state farther north, she jokingly replied, "Prozac, Effexor, Zoloft, Paxil." Though she knew the names of these popular antidepressants, she had not actually used them over the course of her move. Nonetheless, her response resonated and underscored what I'd been hearing all along: Moving is an immensely traumatic experience.

In addition to the physical inconveniences, moving takes a tremendous toll on the psyche. And although feelings and emotions are part of a normal life event, we still are caught off guard. Faced with dueling demons, we are forced to say good-bye, yet are expected to embrace the unknown. Certainly, movement is part of our daily lexicon. Whether we're settling into a new home, changing careers, or assuming a bigger and better title, we just keep going. But how do we remain focused in the midst of so much activity? And, indeed, how do we bid farewell to the past yet maintain an open mind toward the future—a future that cannot possibly live up to what's here and now?

We do it by facing the situation head on. We look at our lives closely and determine what needs careful attention and what may have to be put on hold. If we ignore feelings of loss, for example, they'll only fester and grow larger. Yet dealing with loss doesn't mean wallowing in self-pity. In this chapter, you'll learn how to treat your loss with respect and discover ways to move on.

The Good-bye Tour

During the month preceding our move to the Northeast, my family ventured out on what I termed the "good-bye tour." Every weekend we had dinner with friends who wanted to wish us well, spend one last time together, and, in many cases, review the good old times. After a while these get-togethers began to wear me down. I loved seeing everyone, and I was grateful for their hospitality. But I hated saying good-bye, and I really hated saying it over and over again.

You might be experiencing your own good-bye tour—people calling to wish you well, neighbors wanting to know about the sale of your house, or friends extending invitations for lunch and dinner. Unfortunately, saying good-bye can get short-changed and swept up in the logistics of a move. Make time for proper farewells by doing it your way. For example, saying your good-byes can be the perfect opportunity to take a breather from the hassles of moving. Invite the people you'll miss the most and make it truly special by giving out fun and whimsical moving-away favors:

- Cookie cutters in the shapes of hearts and houses
- Flower seeds and bulbs to plant as a remembrance of your friendship
- Assorted refrigerator magnets that your friends will see every time they reach for a snack

Your gifts don't have to be expensive, just meaningful in small ways. Naturally, you'll want to be gracious if you are invited here and there for final farewells. Bring some of these gifts and attach a special card expressing your gratitude and appreciation for all they've done. Help keep the mood buoyant by speaking hopefully and optimistically about your new locale.

They Miss You, Too

For a while, moving makes you the center of attention. Friends and family hover with questions about how you feel, when you're actually leaving town, and the kind of stove you're inheriting in your new abode. You're showered with invitations to break bread one more time. Eventually, though, you leave and hopefully are missed. And while your friends and family want you to thrive and adjust, they want to be missed as well. Tell them so and remind them that you appreciate their love and support.

For your special friends, the ones who stayed with you through thick and thin, consider giving a gift from the heart— something that will make them say, "Aha! You're so clever!" Here are few ideas:

- A custom-made invitation to lunch at a favorite restaurant
- A box of artistic cards with stamped envelopes preaddressed with your name, street, and town. Attach your own card with a not-so-subtle message such as "I'll miss seeing you, but I can't wait to hear all your news . . ." Include a fancy pen for good measure. (Or split the box among a few special people and tie the cards together with ribbon and a small card for each recipient.)
- Hand-deliver change-of-address cards. Buy prefab cards or make your own. Try using postcards of various landmarks in your new location. (If you can't buy those yourself, call the chamber

of commerce in your new town for an orientation kit; request a stack of postcards, too.)

- Give out prepaid long-distance calling cards (if you've moved out of the area).

Dealing with Loss

Loss is relative. Regardless of who has it better or who has it worse, your loss is valid, true and painful. Uprooting *is* a major upheaval. For some, a move sets into motion a series of losses. One loss reawakens the hurt from an earlier hardship, and the *sense* of loss permeates the air. If you have children, their losses become your own. If you are putting your home up for sale, you face the loss of shelter, of the place that kept you safe. If you've lost a job and must literally move on, you mourn the interruption of a career that must be redirected. On the surface you've lost not only a home but also that part of yourself that is associated with that home. The loss can take on a life of its own, and, very often, the grieving process begins long before an actual move takes place. This is an appropriate response to loss but one that can be managed and overcome.

Knowing a move is on the horizon, you begin to look at things in a different light. "I never really appreciated that grove of trees," you say to yourself. "I should have gone to a play at the university," you scold. "Why didn't I paint the bedroom that shade of gray I like so much?" You might even begin to miss what you never really liked to begin with. "One does not love a place the less for having suffered in it," wrote Jane Austen in *Persuasion*. Rather than a location's beauty, convenience, or other attracting characteristic, it is the habits and expectations you develop that ultimately tie you to one place or another. Your habits, indeed your daily movements, are short-circuited.

Others see life through another lens. "I can't believe you're moving!" they exclaim, or my favorite, "I can't imagine."

These comments are not intended to throw you off guard or push you deeper into an abyss; your friends and family are sad to see you go. Also, not everyone perceives a move as a loss. Coworkers, for instance, may see your move as nothing less than an opportunity. Instead of empathizing with your ambivalence, they may act bewildered, wondering what all the fuss is about. Nonetheless, moving puts people on alert. Arrivals and departures are viewed differently. When someone announces that a move is afoot, we sometimes subconsciously begin to sever ties. We almost allow a certain amount of unraveling to occur. We *disinvest* ourselves of relationships that normally are important. Even the people left behind experience a mobility transference— when the people around them move, they often experience the move vicariously. Their own anchors are pulled up just a bit. Think of shifting ever so slightly the position of a multisided piece of crystal. The crystal itself appears unchanged, yet the light and prisms it casts on a sunny day give a room a totally different look and feel. Similarly, the lives of the people you leave behind are indirectly affected.

So, it's not just moving that makes you sad or feel isolated and alone. It's what a move entails that makes this life change so colossal, so traumatic. What's most striking is the wonder. "Where am I going?" you ask. "Who will I meet? What will life be like? How will I survive?" These questions cannot be answered right away. Moving is an evolutionary process. Like any loss, it takes time and experience to come to terms with the change.

More important is that you recognize that the maelstrom of emotions that envelop you during a course of a move are normal. You may feel shock. You may deny that it's happening and continue on as if nothing at all has changed. You might be angry at being pulled away from what you know and love best. To some degree, you might be afraid of what's next (whatever *next* might be). Even if you want to move, you might be surprised by unanticipated feelings of loss. This is scary stuff and can turn a normally adult-minded person into one who feels silly and childish. Eventually, you will come to understand and accept the realities of a move. Once you reach that point, you can look ahead and truly embrace the possibilities.

Loss of Routine

From the time we are children to our days as adults, we crave and live by routine. Routine keeps us in check. Routine tells us where we're going. Routine offers security; moving interrupts those routines. Moving rocks our world with aftershocks that linger much longer than we'd like.

To keep your routine intact, adhere to certain rules and regulations that, once read and practiced, become second nature—like the steps necessary to obtain a driver's license. Here's how one mover described that experience in his new home state: "[Y]ou can't get a driver's license until you get your car registered; you can't get your car registered until you have state insurance; even after you get the insurance, you still can't get the car registered until it's been inspected, after which you take the green certificate to a county tax office, wait to have your name called, and fork over close to a hundred bucks . . ."

Aside from the obvious frustration of meandering through such a circuitous system, the loss of relying on his old license is quite apparent. Whether it's a new driver's license, arranging for your public utility to turn on the gas and electric, or figuring out the local transportation system, your move undoubtedly will require the creation of a brand-new routine. Once you can slip into a different way of doing things, your old routine—your daily life as you lived it in your previous location—will fade and be replaced by something new and fresh. Follow these three easy steps as you work toward creating a routine you can live with:

1. Truly commit to the new routine.
2. Do what you need to do to achieve your goal.
3. Identify what's working and what's not, and eliminate what's not working.

Developing a new routine, especially as you clear out, pack up, and move in, is no small task. Here are some ways to help you bridge the gap between saying good-bye and then, in another place, saying hello.

Acknowledge your loss. Moving away from all that is familiar is a jolting experience. Accept your feelings for what they are (not for what you or others think they should be) and give yourself permission to grieve.

Accept the ups and downs. Even if you absolutely love change, moving can put anyone in a tailspin. Just when you're feeling pretty low, you get a surge of hope and things don't look so bad after all. While it provides a nice respite for the doom and gloom you might have been experiencing, the euphoric feeling runs its course and then you're back where you started. Understand that this emotional roller coaster is normal and will dissipate over time.

Set realistic goals. Moving and unpacking are difficult enough without your inner voice nagging you to "do this, do that." Do what you can and create an environment that will enhance (not detract from) your ability to achieve your goals. Set specific goals, too, so that there'll be no question as to what you're asking of yourself. Specific achievable goals might be to unpack the kitchen first, then the living room, not to unpack all the boxes within a week.

Live the limbo. The uncertainties inherent in moving keep us painfully in the dark. Is this a big loss or a small loss? Will the house sell? Will you find another place to live? Will you like the new place? Recognize what's within your control and what's not. Then concentrate on what you can control.

Get help if you need it. Don't be shy or proud about getting professional help. If you feel out of control, if you feel lonely with no one to talk to, or if you simply are unsure about how you do feel, muster up the courage to ask for the help you need and deserve.

Remember that you're not alone. In the big picture, you're in the company of millions of other people who move every year. On a smaller scale, lots of people within one community come and go at the same time. Even if you can't talk immediately to someone else who's in your shoes, just knowing that moving is a common phenomenon should give you some peace of mind that others do it and survive it, and so will you.

Give yourself time to adjust. There's no statute of limitations here. Ask five people how long it takes to adjust after a move and you're likely to get as many answers. One woman seated next to me on a plane recently stated unequivocally that it takes at least four years to adapt to and feel comfortable in a new place. It might take you a year (or a year and five months). Everyone struggles with loss on different levels and at different rates. What matters is that you are generous with time and that you give yourself plenty of it.

Clear your plate (or get another from the cupboard). We've become a society that is averse to free time. We fill our plates to the brim, afraid that we might sit idle doing nothing. Goodness knows how important it is to get enough rest and relaxation during the course of a move. Just when you need it the most, energy is in short supply, and no amount of caffeine (which, in large quantities, isn't good for you anyway) or aerobic exercise can substitute for the state of well-being needed during this stressful period. Take a hard look at your plate and move things off if you're overloaded. (Don't move them around, like you did as a kid, moving vegetables here and there for that see-I-ate-some look.) If that's impossible, then take another plate out of the psychic cupboard; that is, carve out a little more time for yourself to get things done. Set priorities and get to what's important first. Don't spread yourself too thin; you will forever be exhausted. Moreover, your perspective and judgment will be clouded.

Recall past triumphs. Remind yourself of the times in your life when you overcame adversity. Assume the role you played then to help you get through what you face today. Be your own best self.

Let family and friends help you out. There's no shame to feeling the tumult of a move. It's okay to seek comfort from the people who mean the most to you. Let them in on what you're experiencing and allow them to offer support. (But politely avoid well-meaning advice givers and try to stick with active listeners— the people less likely to pass judgment on your circumstances and subsequent decisions.)

Ordering Your Life versus Putting Your Life in Order

Part of the upset of moving is facing, head on, the over-whelming task of getting organized. If you're like me, you've accumulated bushel loads of papers, magazines, letters, and other assorted home filler-uppers. Moving is a good time to put your life in order but not to the extent that you create a living pressure cooker.

I have items that just can't seem to find a home—photos waiting to be framed, articles to be filed, magazines to be read. Preparing for a move (or unpacking afterward), these objects turn into real burdens. Setting up an elaborate picture framing system may seem like a good idea. But think about it: Do you really want to saddle yourself with new projects in the midst of a major change? Probably not. If getting organized during a move brings you to your knees, then simply take a break. This is the kind of pressure you don't need. It's okay to feel torn over what may amount to a stack of papers. After all, they're your papers. It's okay to feel confused. This is a confusing time. It's not a good idea, however, to heap more pressure onto your situation. For example, instead of focusing on cataloging photographs into albums, concentrate on your new blank walls and put some pictures up. Order your life according to what you can do in a reasonable amount of time. You can put your life in order after you settle in.

Take a Breather

If you feel as though the rug's been pulled out from under you or you don't know if you're coming or going, take a breather! Most days I try to get outside to walk. Getting away from my work and breathing in some fresh air instantly gives me a new perspective, and it's a great way to fight stress. If you can't get outside, try stopping whatever you're doing and just pause. Then do the following:

- *Breathe deeply.* This will help lower your heart and respiratory rates and clear your mind—a nice bonus.
- *Inhale slowly* to the count of four. Picture the air moving freely to all parts of your body.
- *Exhale slowly* to the count of four. Imagine your stress leaving through the front door.

Continue these breathing exercises a few times before resuming your activities. Practice this exercise with regularity. It helps; you'll see.

Taking Care

It is a natural human impulse to take care of and be cared for by others. Caretaking heals, energizes, and propels us forward. Unfortunately, caretaking is diminished during the course of a move. Unpacking boxes, learning your way around, managing your family's adjustment (spouse, kids, dogs, cats) and trying hard to belong sap your physical and emotional reserves. As a newcomer, you're not likely to be cared for in the way you might have been in your previous location (especially if you had extended family around). Not at first, anyway.

Replenishing your reserves is especially critical as you uproot and take stock of what you're leaving behind and what may be in the future. Moving is a disruption. To treat it otherwise is to short-change your experience. Pampering yourself may seem like a luxury. But if you want to have energy, if you want to be optimistic, if you want the move to be successful, you must take care of yourself. I gained seven pounds in the week that we moved. I was not taking care of myself. Eating pizza on move-in day is a great convenience; ordering it every night for a week will give you heartburn. You may fall off your exercise regimen for a day or two. Giving it up entirely or until you "have the time" isn't smart. So at the end of each day ask, "Did I take care of myself today?" If you answer yes, you'll be a better colleague, a better partner, a better parent, and most important, a better person. And you'll have a better transition.

Keep a Settling-In Journal

Keeping a journal is a constructive way to diffuse stress and manage a loss. Journaling is especially useful if you prefer to keep feelings to yourself. Pen your own narrative and include those feelings, observations, hopes, and anything else that needs to be expressed. No editing or second drafts are necessary. This private correspondence is for your eyes only. Here are a few guidelines for keeping your settling-in journal:

- *Keep it simple.* Don't feel obligated to make long, involved entries on a daily basis. Write what you can, when you can.
- *Treat yourself to a decorative journal.* Many stationery and book stores stock a variety of blank-paged writing journals.

- *Include small and large triumphs.* If you've had a good day, describe it in celebratory detail. You'll revel in your successes as you review the pages at a later date.
- *Document defeat.* What better place to vent your frustration than in a private journal?
- *Express gratitude.* For each entry, try to include at least two things you're grateful for—for example, the neighbor who welcomed you with a plate of cookies, the supermarket that carries your favorite brand of jam.
- *Throw in a few goals.* Occasionally include what you'd like to accomplish, from the mundane to the exciting—for example, a visit to the public library, volunteering for a worthy cause, remodeling your charming yet outdated kitchen.

The Next Best Thing

The telephone used to be the "next best thing to being there." Today, we have e-mail with its instant messages and inexpensive transmission. But it doesn't compare to the comfort of a familiar voice. Staying in touch with old friends and others left behind can actually boost your efforts toward acclimating to your new environment. It's not unreasonable to set aside funds to pay for long-distance telephone calls. If you really want to hear your phone ring, consider installing a toll-free number for your VIPs. Expect to pay a nominal monthly fee along with a per-minute rate.

An Anchor Wherever You Are

Moving is more than physically transferring your belongings from one place to another. Moving is a process—a process of saying good-bye, creating closure, and then finally making a new place for yourself. It's true that even some of your beloved objects won't survive a move. What does survive will last a lifetime—your values, your meaningful relationships, and the support of your loved ones. These are your anchors.

Your anchors make you authentic, your own person with a destiny to choose. Whenever you leave familiar surroundings, you carry with you the inherited wisdom of your past. Rely on this wisdom and use your anchors to help you overcome the upheaval and, later, embrace the changes that a move inevitably brings.

Don't be surprised if your anchors materialize out of thin air. A few months after moving, I found an anchor in the airwaves. Visiting with a friend one afternoon, I heard in the background the familiar voices from National Public Radio. "I didn't know we had a public radio station here," I confessed. "Oh, sure," said my friend as she wrote down the call letters and the frequency. That evening I went home, tuned in, and felt more connected to the community than I had in weeks. What turned out to be a simple turn of the dial became a significant moment in time. As I listened to the broadcast, I marveled at the familiar voice that from several hundred miles away made my place start to feel like home. I still had lots of settling in to do, but I knew from that point on that in spite of this peripatetic life, I would grow new roots and thrive.

Taking Inventory

- Say good-bye on your own terms.
- Acknowledge and respect your feelings of loss.
- Set realistic goals.
- Write down your feelings and impressions.
- Create your own anchors.

Chapter 2

Moving and Working: Maintaining the Momentum

The simple idea that everyone needs a reasonable amount
of challenging work in his or her life, and also a
personal life . . . has never really taken hold.

—Judith Martin, *Common Courtesy*

Work is often an overlooked but critical part of the moving experience for singles and couples. Most people who relocate do so because of a job transfer within their existing companies, a need to find work, or to take a new job in another location. In its *1998 Survey of Corporate Relocation Policies,* Atlas Van Lines reported that 40.7 percent of companies' "average transferees" relocated once every three to five years. Runzheimer International (Rochester, Wisconsin) describes the typical transferee as a white male, age 35 to 45 years, with two children.

While the person who relocates with a job in hand usually has the benefit of a schedule, a structure, and a central focus, he or she must still contend with the stress that permeates a relocation. The relocating partner may suddenly be back in the job market. Can your personal and professional lives coexist against the backdrop of a move?

In this chapter, you'll learn how to rank your priorities, handle the stress of a new job, and work collaboratively with your employer to achieve a smooth transition. Relocating partners will learn how to network and land a job (or find consulting work) in the new location.

An Industry Snapshot

Corporate support—financial and otherwise—can have tremendous impact on your transition success. Or if you're an entrepreneur starting a new company or moving your old one, brisk sales may be enough to call your move a victory.

Your reasons for moving also play a significant role in how you approach a move. A promotion (including salary increase) accompanying a move to a desirable spot sets a different tone than a relocation that's been forced by downsizing. Returning to hometown territory to care for an aging parent presents still another set of issues that will influence your transition.

In the past, transferring employees or relocating new hires was a common and essential part of conducting business. And workers, reluctant to turn down gainful employment, accepted relocation as a normal component of building or at least maintaining a career. Today, however, the numbers of domestic transfers are going down. According to the *1997 Survey and Analysis of Employee Relocation Policies and Costs,* conducted every two years by Runzheimer International, the average number of domestic transfers per company dropped nearly 50 percent from 232 in 1986 to 133 in 1996. The improved job market—at least in some parts of the country—is one reason for the drop. If you're a top performer in high demand, you probably can afford to be more selective as you tap into various employment opportunities. A precarious corporate climate (What corporation isn't unsteady?) may preclude you from moving across country for a job that might be abolished within six months. Industry experts attribute the drop to increased layoffs (fewer workers to transfer), corporate cost-cutting measures, and family-conscious employees who question relocation as a necessary career strategy. Some executives are even opting to commute long distances instead of moving outright. Indeed, Atlas Van Lines' *1998 Survey of Corporate Relocation Policies* reported nearly three-quarters of the employers surveyed cited family ties as the main reason employees turn down transfers.

Still, people continue to move. Some of us simply don't have the luxury to choose. Whether you've been downsized, rightsized, or reengineered out of a job, you're likely to follow the money. If you're single, particularly without children, you may have less to lose and therefore take the risk. If your loved ones are scattered all over the country or the world, family ties may not be an issue. Of if you're married and don't have kids rooted in a particular school system, you may be more inclined to try something (and someplace) new. And what about those once-in-a-lifetime opportunities that you simply can't turn down?

Beyond Financial Support

In some ways, transferees are simply more truthful. In the 80s, people talked about the importance of spousal assistance. In the 90s, workers cite cost of living as a barrier to relocating. More recently, though, people are speaking more truthfully about issues like work and family balance and job satisfaction. Some companies, of course, are more open to family concerns than others. Creating workplaces that are supportive of the *whole* person—work, family, community involvement—and environments in which workers feel free to air concerns such as how their families might fare during the course of a relocation is making it easier for employers to attract good people and for those people to find happiness in their professional lives.

Are You Statistically Equal?

How do you compare with the typical transferee? In 1997, this individual had the following characteristics:

Age
Less than 35 years old—43%
35 to 45 years old—53%
Over 45 years old—4%

Marital Status
Married—75%
Single—25%

Number of Children
None—10%
One child—20%
Two children—50%
Two children—50%
Three or more children—20%

In the same year, the *atypical* transferee looked like this:
Women—26%
Ethnic minorities—12%
Single parents—10%
Primary caregivers for elderly parents—7%

Source: *Runzheimer Reports on Relocation,* May 1998, Vol. 17, No. 3.

"But I Thought You Said . . ."

Missed communications, incorrect assumptions, ultimate disappointments. Unless you fully understand your company's relocation policies—including financial and other types of support—you risk misinterpreting what your employer is willing to provide. What the company considers sufficient may seem inadequate to

City Sneak Preview

Companies courting prospective employees know that they're selling more than the corporate cafeteria. They want their prospective employees to buy into the whole community. At Bausch & Lomb, a program is in the works to introduce serious job candidates to Rochester, New York, giving them the chance to evaluate the community before actually moving there. Even companies that do not have such programs may be willing to contract out this responsibility to destination services—firms that have special expertise in showing prospective newcomers an unfamiliar area—in order to ensure your (and your family's) comfort level regarding the new location. An incompatible location can cancel out the benefits of a stellar job offer. It's best to know as much as you can before you make the leap.

Even companies that do not have extensive experience relocating their employees can be instrumental in the transition process. It may just mean allowing employees to do what's necessary to settle themselves and their families, if they have them. It may also mean that you need to do what's important for you—asking your supervisor for additional time to help your family get settled, doing what you can to keep your priorities on track so you can concentrate on the job. If you're traveling a lot as your family is settling in, consider a good calling card program. Staying in touch is key.

you. In order to avoid this scenario, ask up front for clarification of the company's policies. Also, be prepared to maintain open and steady communication with all of the people involved in the move—representatives from recruiting, relocation, and human resources management. But remember to do your homework: Read the material and be forthright with any questions you have. You'll alleviate a lot of problems down the road by familiarizing yourself with everyone's role in the transition process—not just your own.

Still, depending on your personality and your employer, initiating concerns over transfers—domestic and international—carries a certain degree of risk. Say you've relocated and six months down the road, after the excitement has worn off, your spouse hasn't found employment and your kids haven't made new friends. For many workers, midlevel and executives alike, there is a stigma attached to sharing personal information—the corporate equivalent to "airing your dirty laundry." Some companies are farther along in their efforts to adopt work-family programs and policies. On the other hand, if your company does not have a history of being family-friendly, it's not likely to suddenly take on specific work-family issues. So, be cautious as you air your concerns. It's best to check around and find others with whom you can align.

Many of us can relate to what can happen if we express a grievance in one lone voice. Sometimes nothing happens. Other times we may lose credibility or a prominent place on the organization chart. Building allies, especially those with some organizational clout, can in time diffuse a personal grievance into a progressive corporate policy. Some people still have difficulty admitting they have children, fearing their supervisors will question their commitment to the job. If you can't pinpoint your company's policy toward helping families adjust to relocations, seek out others who have come before you. Ask how management perceives the transition period and ferret out strategies that have resulted in positive outcomes for everyone involved. And remember that ultimately it's in your employer's best interest to help you get through the ups and downs that are inevitable with major change.

A common avenue for workers seeking help is a company's employee assistance program (EAP). The problem with going the EAP route is the perceived lack of privacy and confidentiality, because it is administered by the employer. And regardless of the ways internal services can genuinely improve someone's situation, an employee seeking counsel through an EAP may be seen as broken or weak, unable to handle the job. Many human resources experts acknowledge the difficulties that workers encounter as they consider their options regarding EAPs. Some corporate relocation managers report that a lot of people don't want to expose their weaknesses. Ruth Davis, manager of relocation services for Johnson & Johnson, says that the grief over the death of a loved one is probably more accepted among a worker's peers than is the despair or other hardships that may occur as a result of relocation.

Job Change Strategies That Work

Changing jobs is stressful enough. Add a relocation to the equation and you've got some heavy-hitting anxiety to contend with. Unfortunately, change in the workplace has become so pervasive that we've lost sight of its harmful effects. "Get over it" may be a popular admonition, but for most people, mastering change requires something a little more strategic. When a social worker friend of mine left a position at a large teaching hospital in Washington, D.C., to work in a clinic in Louisville, Kentucky, her entire professional career underwent a significant rebirth. Her new colleagues' different work styles at first made her feel like an outsider, especially since few support systems were in place to help her with the transition. Sometimes she had to resist the temptation to apologize for who she was and wondered whether she should have changed in order to fit in.

Fitting in is especially important when you're new, and while my friend had, and has, full confidence in her abilities, she is not unlike a lot of us who might question our professional identities when we begin something new. You might ask yourself, "Should I adjust my thinking?" "Is my style too traditional/progressive?" "How should I behave?" These are not bad questions to ask. But if answering them begins to chip away at your self-esteem, then it's probably time to remind yourself of why you were hired in the first place. As an outsider, you will at first be viewed as an agent of change. Just as you will need to adjust to your colleagues' work styles, they, too, will need time to adapt to whatever you're bringing to the table—skills, talents, and faults.

Focus on the opportunities instead of those nagging and distracting risks by applying these strategies:

- *Don't fight it.* Understand your employer's expectations and see how well they align with your own.
- *Remove the pressure.* Accepting change doesn't occur overnight. Give it time.
- *Play up your strengths.* Rather than focus on what you *can't* do, concentrate on your skills and the qualities that set you apart from the pack.
- *Practice diplomacy and maintain positive relationships.* This applies to most situations, but is especially useful for the new kid on the block.
- *Seek out a comrade (or two) at work in whom you can confide.* Look for someone who's "been there" and has survived to tell about it. But don't divulge too much information.
- *Be optimistic (fake it if you have to).* Just acting hopeful and open-minded can help people adapt. Just keep repeating to yourself: "Opportunity, opportunity, opportunity."

Corporate Response

Even with companies cutting back on their relocation perks, many are crafting packages to retain and attract the best and brightest. Still, these moves are not cheap. In 1996, the Employee

Relocation Council (ERC) reported that the average cost of relocating a current homeowning employee and a new hire was $47,901 and $37,671, respectively. Many in corporate America recognize the benefits of providing emotional and financial support for its nomadic employees. Transferees who have trouble adjusting to their new surroundings may not perform well on the job. Even those who are relatively happy and good at acclimating to new communities (and corporate cultures) are not immune to the effects relocation has on a spouse or children. This is especially true for international assignments. In the long run, a failed transfer—when workers return home prematurely—usually costs a company more than the original investment to relocate an employee.

Bolstering corporate relocation activity are the many consulting, or third-party, companies set up to take care of a host of moving tasks from house selling to new city orientations. The Impact Group, a St. Louis–based national relocation service, counsels families on schools, provides information on entertainment, and can even locate a veterinarian for the family pet.

It's clear from numerous interviews with relocation professionals that corporate America recognizes the value of providing support that transcends financial packages. By providing adequate counseling, intercultural training, and other services designed to ease the transition, companies are more likely to see returns on their personnel-related investments. Through the efforts of its Expatriate Management Committee, the National Foreign Trade Council (NFTC) is helping its member companies create environments in which prospective employees initiate transfers, a self-election process that could reduce the number of failed assignments.

How companies respond to changing demographics will have a profound effect on how well they attract and retain their best and brightest. And as their many talented employees fuse their personal values with their approaches to work, companies will need to create work environments that are supportive and respectful of their employees. This will be especially true as the typical transferee population becomes more diversified. Women, ethnic minorities, single parents, and those charged with elder-care are changing the workplace, forcing companies to reexamine their policies and programs. Relocation professionals will continue to educate themselves so that they can accommodate this societal shift. They'll conduct and sponsor studies, attend conferences and workshops, and read up on what's happening in human resources management. But the rest will be up to you. You must communicate your needs and concerns. You must raise objections and work toward mutually beneficial solutions.

International Moves: Beyond the Adventure

While the number of corporate domestic moves may be down, an increasingly competitive global market is contributing to a surge in international assignments. The success of an expatriate is crucial; without it a U.S. firm's interest in a foreign market can spiral downward, resulting in lost revenues and possibly even plant closures. Overseas assignments may conjure up exotic cultures, old-world charm, and exciting destinations. Yet unlike vacations, working abroad is exactly that: work. But the work encompasses much more than the technical aspects of a job, especially if you've brought along a spouse or children. Indeed, many workers refuse to live abroad out of concern for their spouses' careers and for their kids. On the other hand, one-third of the companies surveyed by the ERC in 1997 expected to see an increase in international relocation in the next five years. Indeed, in the past one out of 18 relocation assignments at Intel Corporation was for an international position. In the late 1990s, one out of five moves is for an overseas assignment, according to Patricia Nealon, Intel's manager of worldwide relocation.

In spite of a growing global economy and an adventurous spirit among some workers, expatriates continue to suffer for a multitude of reasons. A spouse may not be able to find work. A single worker may not be well versed in rules for dating. Children may miss their friends "back home." Cultural nuances can get in the way of everyday business matters. In short, the worker and his or her family may never adjust. Concern over family members may distract a worker from his or her job, resulting in poor performance. Smart companies can usually identify a problem before it becomes unmanageable. Cornelius Grove of Cornelius Grove & Associates LLC, calls the lackluster performance and its damaging effects a brownout. "If someone is preoccupied with spousal issues, for example, or is having trouble assimilating, he or she may not perform at a level that is consistent with company goals. It's like an interruption in the electrical source for a lightbulb; instead of burning bright and constant, it flickers and becomes a distraction."

Grove's remarks underscore the importance of providing pre-departure assistance and continuous support for expatriates and their families. In many instances, the problems that arise with international assignments go beyond the obvious cultural differences. Our domestic perspective on teamwork, for example, may not translate halfway around the world. Likewise, our sense of time (hurried for most American businesses) may, understandably, not be in sync with counterparts 4,000 miles away. When cross-cultural issues have a negative impact on performance, people, products, and systems get tangled up. Companies that address these issues head-on are more likely to minimize brownout. They're also in a better position to decrease the number of failed transfers.

One Foot In, One Foot Out

Claudia, who recently returned to the U.S. after a two-year stint in London, says she never felt fully connected to her community in England. A human resources director for an international investment bank, she recalls certain experiences that prevented her from truly setting down roots. She became technically proficient in no time, but learning how to conduct herself in a different culture took longer. Buying vegetables and fruits in an open market became a lesson in appropriate consumer behavior. Common, everyday occurrences—traveling on the subway, shopping, handling money—did not come naturally to Claudia. Certainly, learning how to deal with the daily stuff of living takes a lot of energy. It's not something you can shrug off. Your colleagues "back home" may think you're off setting business precedents. But it takes tremendous fortitude to be an international trailblazer, even if your host country is English-speaking.

Though Claudia describes her experience as one in which she felt she had one foot in and one foot out, she still considers herself a better person for the experience, much stronger and more flexible. My guess is that she's a very effective human resources professional as well.

The National Foreign Trade Council, which advocates international business and trade, is working with some of its members to improve the expatriate's experience. The NFTC's Bill Fontana, whose own résumé includes ten years working for Citibank in Athens, London, Bangkok, and Jakarta, says that many expatriates unknowingly are viewed as a threat to their peers and even supervisors, sometimes simply because the home office doesn't understand the depth of what this employee has accomplished overseas.

Itinerary for Success

Once you've agreed to an international assignment, start thinking about what *you* can do (instead of waiting for your company to do) to ensure the highest probability for success. The following tips will help you skipper the high seas of global relocation.

Recognize up-front the magnitude of the adjustment. Just because you've done it before, or you're known for your high level of achievement, don't underestimate the time it takes to understand even the smallest challenge that foreign travel may present.

Determine before you leave how your employer plans to capitalize on your expatriate experience. There's no rule preventing you from working with your employer—early on—to create a career path that will take advantage of your overseas experience. This will help you and your employer to view your time abroad as a continuation of rather than an interruption in your career.

Ask for help. If employer assistance is not forthcoming, take the lead and ask for assistance in understanding local customs and knowing what is acceptable or taboo, among other things.

Redirect well-intentioned efforts. If you are receiving assistance that actually *impedes* your adjustment, raise the issue and offer an alternative.

Maintain steady communications with a colleague back home. Informal communication is essential in today's fast-paced business environment, especially if you're away from the home office. Keep tabs on your company's stateside corporate culture by staying in close touch with a trusted associate who serves as your conduit with headquarters.

Keep reading about your host country. It's easy to get swept up in the maelstrom of an overseas assignment. Good intentions give way to deadlines, paperwork, and finally, the flight out. If you began reading about your destination prior to departure, stay with it even after you've arrived. It will help put things in perspective and increase your ability to adapt. To your hosts, it will demonstrate your commitment to and respect for their culture. This goes for your business associates as well as your neighbors.

Make sure your family receives adequate preparation and ongoing support. Intercultural training that your employer considers *de rigueur* for you may seem optional or even unnecessary for your family. Help with language, for example, should at the very least be part of your relocation package. The speed at which you adjust to another culture is directly related to how well you understand and communicate with others. Without that you are literally lost, particularly in a medical emergency. In addition, ask your employer to help you and your family understand the local culture and business climate.

Quitting Time on Your Terms

When Michelle learned that her husband would be taking a job in the Middle East, she quit her management position at a Fortune 500 company. That was a big mistake, she says. Obtaining the proper paperwork took longer than expected, so she ended up staying back in the states for another six months before she and her husband were reunited. The separation, coupled with extra time on her hands, made the situation worse. In retrospect, Michelle says she would have held onto her job, giving notice closer to the real date of her departure.

Even with these tips and the safety net provided by your employer, your intercultural thermostat may require occasional adjustments. For many people, relocating to a foreign land is simply a greater challenge than the one that takes you from Maine to Virginia. Until you can grasp the language, for example, you're constantly at the mercy of someone else.

Mary, a Xerox executive whose travels have taken her from hometown beginnings in New Zealand to three U.S. cities, Australia, France, and 15 countries in Africa, knows that it takes time to assimilate. As a result, she does not pressure herself to feel at home at the start. In the past, she viewed a 6- to 12-month stint as a business trip, not a move. This, too, has removed some of the pressure.

Repatriation: Preparing for Your Homecoming

Returning home after living abroad is a far cry from the re-entry one might experience after vacationing in another country. What for years seemed familiar may suddenly feel foreign and unusual. The time you need to readjust will vary depending on the duration of your assignment. If you've been away for more than a year, for example, you might notice dramatic changes in the city to which you are returning. And if you're returning with kids whose adolescence was spent overseas, you'll need to help them cope with their new environment. Claudia, the human resources director, described her homecoming as one of relearning. "You lose your cultural references, whether you're coming or going," she says. "It really takes some time to get grounded. You're not sure where you belong."

The best strategy is to prepare for your departure long before you've handed the flight attendant your airline ticket. Just as you presumably prepared for your trip abroad, you can easily begin the process of reentry with a little planning and preparation. Take advantage of any assistance your employer can provide, but don't give up if your company has no formal repatriation program. Instead, simply ask what kinds of outside resources might be available. And if you're unhappy with the arrangements that your company has set up for finding housing, for example, stand up and be heard, but do so politely and without an attitude. Employers tend to frown on arrogant demands. Instead of approaching your employer with a list of terms and conditions for your return, engender a sense of goodwill by offering a compromise. If your company has given you eight days to find a new home and transportation, ask if the time might be extended by a week or two. If after you return you find that things are not working to your satisfaction, revisit the agreement originally drawn up between you and your employer. Not all arrangements are set in stone. Bottom-line your situation, emphasizing that the support you receive will enhance your productivity and ultimately hasten your adjustment.

Some consulting firms, like Cornelius Grove & Associates, specialize in repatriation and coaching. A counselor with cross-cultural expertise may also ease your transition. If you are reluctant to ask for help or consider counseling a "personal" issue unrelated to your performance at work, think again. Although you may have experienced tremendous professional and personal growth overseas, you may not know how to integrate your new perspective into the home office environment. You may also confront a corporate culture that's different from the one you left. Worse, you may encounter resistance by colleagues who may be slow to recognize your new skill set. Some colleagues may feel threatened by your global knowledge, especially those who might have wanted the experience as well but for various reasons stayed behind. Plus, if the authority you exercised abroad has been downgraded, you're likely to feel frustrated and even a little demoralized.

Enlisting the support of a mentor in the home office is a great way to expedite the debriefing process. Grove reminds returning expatriates to ask themselves, "How can I put this recent enhancement of my knowledge, skill, and wisdom to work on behalf of career, company, community, and family?" As with any change, try to view your return as an opportunity for further growth. Along the way you'll need to identify impediments and then strategies to overcome whatever is preventing forward movement.

Ready, Set, Succeed

Even if relocating was not your choice, it *is* possible to succeed in your new workplace. Much of this book focuses on the benefits of exuding a positive attitude. Doing so in your new work environment will keep you fresh, help you learn, and demonstrate to others that you're willing to be a team member. All of this will go a long way toward making your transition one you can live with. Enhance your adjustment by following these simple tips.

Practice good listening skills. This is a tried and true method of winning the respect of your colleagues. Quite simply, it demonstrates your interest in what others have to say.

Create several networking opportunities. Don't rely solely on your immediate work group; stretch and try to meet people in other places—at special work-sponsored events, in the company cafeteria. Take advantage of being the newcomer; many folks like to take recent arrivals under their wings.

Ask questions, observe, and listen. Don't be afraid of appearing clueless if you're not sure of something. A new job— even one with the same company—comes with a whole new set of rules and expectations. Asking questions, listening to the answers, and observing what goes on around you are the best ways to gather intelligence.

Move forward. Settling into a new job is the perfect breeding ground for comparisons. New faces and different policies may have you pining for your old job. Look for new ways to approach situations and consider the opinions of your coworkers who have the benefit of more time and experience in the new workplace.

Make allowances for hard work. What new job doesn't require an immense amount of time and dedication? The exhaustion from moving, however, can sap the energy you need to put in the 200 percent your employer expects. Do what you can—a few minutes of meditation, eating a balanced diet, leaving work at the office on Friday nights—to ward off burnout.

You Can *Take It with You*

What if you're moving your business but want to maintain a presence in your old location? What about the person who'd like to keep the job but must first pitch management about the virtues of telecommuting? Both scenarios occur with increasing frequency every day. Precise planning, extra time, and a tenacious spirit can make it happen for you as well.

Robert, a business consultant, keeps two clocks on his desk. One keeps him in sync with his clients in Portland, Oregon. The other helps him maintain his East Coast schedule. After moving from Portland after his wife started a new job in upstate New York, Robert was determined to continue servicing his Portland customers while he cultivated new business in and around upstate New York.

He left Portland with every intention of servicing his clients there in the same way he had done before. He did give them the option, however, of taking their business elsewhere, but with one exception, Robert managed to keep each account. It was then his job to make himself easily accessible to his clients.

In order to maintain a presence in Portland *and* provide his clients a familiar and convenient way to stay in touch, Robert kept his original seven-digit number, adding a remote call-forwarding feature. (Callers still paid for a local call.) This enabled him to keep his geographic distance somewhat transparent, though it's no secret that he's in another state. The perception, however, is that he's not that far away. Monthly visits out west, combined with his original phone number, give his clients a sense that he is still reachable and committed to their business. For Robert, it's become the best of two worlds.

Some business advisers recommend using a toll-free number, depending on your location and objective. According to my telephone company sources, that may be a cheaper way to go. For Robert, however, the "if it ain't broke, don't fix it" adage has yielded the best results. He's relied on remote call forwarding instead of a toll-free number, which would have required his Oregon clients and prospects to learn a new number and dial additional digits. He's convinced it works because he continues to get new business from the Portland area.

Be There, Do That

When a consultant's accessibility dips, his or her income may do the same. Avoid this scenario by doing the following:

- Establish a Web home page with a permanent domain or Internet address.
- Make sure your contact information listed with your professional affiliations is current (if the organization maintains a Web directory, be sure to check its accuracy regarding your entry).
- Get creative by establishing some permanent point of access for your clients, readers, whomever.

And don't forget about the utility of e-mail. Although the clocks keep him straight, he must still respect the three-hour time difference, especially when Portland is sleeping. Robert admits that it's frustrating to stay off the phone but respects his clients' personal lives, and, as a result, relies on e-mail to relay messages so that he's not calling at strange hours.

For Robert, the 3,000-mile move forced him to reexamine his market and the strategies he employs to reach that market. Until he moved, he didn't realize that his business could expand the way it has. In addition to exploring the New York market, Robert has cultivated clients from Washington, D.C., the Midwest, and Alaska. If he'd stayed in Portland, he may never have won those contracts.

Here are some other strategies that you can apply to your own move:

- Introduce yourself and your services through a well-planned media blitz. When speaking with the media, be sure to enlist their help in sharing any information that will help you understand this new market.
- Try to get your name (or your company's) published in your local newspaper or regional magazine. Familiarize yourself completely with the publications you're interested in approaching. Make sure you understand the publications' editorial guidelines before submitting a query or a complete article.
- Seek out speaking opportunities in your new location. This will showcase your services, speed up your credibility among the locals, and provide a natural outlet for networking.
- Get to know the key players in your industry and ferret out any opportunities that will enable you to collaborate.
- Be a resource for others. As you develop your roster of people-in-the-know, be magnanimous and share the information with others. This is a great way to position yourself as an expert.
- Accept the fact that you're starting over and in some measure will need to prove yourself all over again. As a seasoned professional, establishing yourself in a new city can be a humbling experience. This should not preclude you from pursuing your market aggressively. What's important is to carefully straddle both sides of the fence. You can promote yourself effectively, but you must do so with an almost irreverent respect for the environment around you. For example, making subtle references to your past accomplishments is a pleasant and non-

threatening way to attract interest in your business (without compromising your goals).

It didn't occur to Sharon, a multimedia expert, to leave her job just because she was moving out of state. When her fiancé landed a job at Michigan State University, she knew she'd need to move away from her company's headquarters. But she liked her job and was highly motivated to work out some kind of mutually beneficial arrangement.

Face Time

There's nothing like face-to-face contact for getting your point across. Or for others to connect a face, a name, and a voice in the same room. If you're telecommuting, however, "face time" usually takes a back seat. And if your colleagues aren't accustomed to communicating in other ways (video teleconferencing, e-mail), then it's especially challenging to stay in touch. Give your coworkers time to adjust to the new arrangement. Remind them about how much you appreciate their support and try to accommodate their schedules as much as possible. It may require more investment on your part, but you're likely to reap larger-than-usual dividends.

Sharon's research revealed the availability, right in East Lansing, of a high-speed cable modem service that would enable her to telecommute with the home office. Her employer met her somewhat unconventional proposal with a cautious but open mind. Most people are taken off the routing list when a departure is imminent, yet the multimedia presentations company that employed Sharon didn't want to lose a valuable employee, someone in whom they'd invested a great amount of time and money.

In fact, it probably would have cost more to replace her with someone new.

Companies that offer telecommuting arrangements must, with their employees, create a relationship based on trust. Sharon's successful six-year track record with the company put to rest any reservations about her off-site presence. Nonetheless, management there still needed to contend with the feelings of other employees who also may have wanted to enjoy this flexible work arrangement. Encountering resistance from fellow workers is probably normal and, over time, tends to dissipate. Recognize that others might not share your enthusiasm as you work toward a mutually beneficial telecommuting arrangement.

For Sharon, the experiment succeeded. Within the first eight months of the new arrangement, she was promoted to manager of Internet development. Be on the lookout for similar opportunities. With more and more high-speed modem cable services becoming available around the country, saying good-bye to a good job may not be necessary.

Entrepreneur versus Corporate Mover

Do you prefer the freedom of calling your own shots or the corporate culture that keeps you surrounded by coworkers and a steady hum of office politics? Often people relocate with the intention of working but at the onset are not certain about how the work will be manifested. If you've always dreamed of being your own boss, moving to a new place could be the perfect opportunity for you to actualize your professional dreams. On the other hand, if corporate camaraderie keeps you centered, then a steady job in-house is probably the best choice.

Here are some questions to ask yourself to help you decide where you might fall on the working continuum:

- Do I need the relative security and community that an office job provides?
- Do I thrive on creativity and flexibility?
- Am I capable of selling myself or do I prefer to rely on an employer to do it for me?
- Can I afford to be my own boss?
- Do I even know what kind of business I'd like to own?

These questions are really intended to trigger your feelings about work—where, what kind, and when. Whatever you decide, don't make the mistake of waiting for something to hit you at the right time. Be proactive, create a business plan, consult with the experts. Don't wait for the perfect opportunity to fall into your lap.

After their daughter was born, Carolyn and her husband made a conscious decision to drop out of the corporate world to pursue ownership of a franchise. A franchise, they reasoned, would provide the flexibility they needed as parents and replace the financial security they previously enjoyed with steady paychecks. After scoping out several areas, they settled on a city in upstate New York. They've had moderate success in the business and look forward to helping it grow. The social aspects of the move, however, have left Carolyn somewhat disappointed and a little dazed. After graduating from college, she moved to wherever the opportunities arose. Everything was new and the excitement of constant change filled her with energy. She was also single and didn't have children. Surprised by how much time and effort she's had to invest in the move, she plans to take some time to work with her husband to stabilize the business. Then she'll turn her attention on her social life and begin to make inroads into the community.

If your move entails opening a business, consider small ways in which you might create a social life that can coexist with your work life. Waiting until your business is up and running is a laudable goal. But the isolation is burdensome and may even prolong the time it takes to establish your business. Carolyn longs for a support group to which she can vent and listen to others living under similar circumstances. If, like Carolyn, you cannot justify the time needed to invest in social and work relationships, consider the value that these ties can give to your business. Toughing it out for an entire year may in the long-term lead to a costly and painful bout of burnout. Do yourself and your business a favor by infusing your life with a few activities that are separate from the day-to-day routine.

Help for Relocating Partners

After my husband and I relocated, I welcomed the chance to take a breather from the daily grind of a full-time job. I had worked for almost ten straight years and relished the idea of setting down roots for myself and my family without the rigors and pressures of a new job. Within our first year, I even considered forgoing a career to care for my daughter full-time.

Rolodex in Rhapsody

Donna, an independent writer/producer who's relocated with her husband more than once, asks everyone she meets to open up their Rolodex and share the names of others whom she might contact as business prospects. "Even if people aren't hiring or don't need me to write a script, they are more than happy to give me their contacts," she says.

At one point I tried to convince myself that maybe I didn't want to work after all. Who wanted to look for a job anyway? And besides, where would I start? So when people asked me what I was doing in terms of my career, I'd say I was "getting the lay of the land," trying to understand how the city operated. The truth was that I really wanted to work, but I couldn't seem to create a plan of action. I was clearly demonstrating self-defeating behaviors. Eventually I took a full-time position with an advertising agency, where I remained for about a year before I started my own marketing communications business. While I gained tremendous experience, I may have reaped greater professional rewards if I had just planned ahead and used the job-searching resources that are so prevalent today.

Whether you need to work for financial reasons or for self-esteem purposes (or both), it's critical to create a strategy that will help you achieve your professional goals and objectives. Waiting for the "right thing to come along" should not be in your professional vernacular. The bottom line is this: If working makes you feel more whole, then finding a job (or starting your own company) will enhance your ability to become more comfortable with and acclimated to your new community.

Long-Distance Jumpers

If relocating means a new job for you as well as for your spouse, you may opt to look for work prior to the actual move. Frank, a night-shift supervisor for a commercial testing laboratory, inquired about, interviewed for, and subsequently accepted a position before even arriving at his new location. Once he knew that he and his wife were moving, Frank immediately began networking through his professional association. "I looked in the directory of the American Association of Blood Banks for organizational members located in or near Phoenix," explains Frank. "I composed a cover letter that outlined my goals and began sending resumés to those places that piqued my interest."

Apply Today!

It's never too late to join a trade or professional association geared to individuals in your field. These groups are always in hot pursuit of new members. But don't wait until you've moved to sign up. Memberships can normally be transferred from one location to another, so you only have to write a check once. The idea is to get on board as soon as possible and begin taking advantage of the resources that so many organizations offer (networking, job listings, professional enhancement, and continuing education, among others).

Frank followed up each correspondence with a telephone call. Eventually, he hooked up with a company that hired him based on his written representation and a series of long-distance telephone interviews. Ironically, it was through another company that did not have openings that Frank landed his new job. "A woman from one company that did not have openings referred me to someone she knew at another firm that was hiring," he says. "That company wasn't even on my original list."

As you assemble your own system for finding a job, apply these long-distance tactics as well:

- Tap into your partner's company spousal assistance program. Find out if the company has any resources to make your transition a smooth one. Will the company pay for a job-finder's fee? Can you get a job within the company? Does the company offer job placement support? Will human resources help you land a job elsewhere?
- Go online and check out the Web sites of the companies located in your new destination.

- Research your new city's business activity by reading every newspaper and magazine article you can find. Searching for these at your local library should be a cinch.
- Focus on the number and kinds of jobs available in your field (or at least in the fields you're considering). Remember that a skill set that is in hot demand in one area may not be marketable in another. Nothing is universal.
- Launch a rigorous networking schedule. That means asking everyone you know if they know someone in your new destination who might be able to help you in your job search.
- Update your resumé and have plenty of copies on hand to distribute.
- Request a packet of information from your new location's chamber of commerce.
- Keep a list of names, addresses, and telephone numbers of everyone you contact. You'll need those to send thank-you notes and for any other follow-up.
- Contact your college alumni office for names, addresses, and phone numbers of fellow alumni living in your new location. Then write to them stating clearly your objectives.
- If you can swing it, plan a job-searching trip prior to the move. Try to schedule as many informational interviews as possible.
- Subscribe to your new city's largest daily newspaper and any business publications. Make a commitment to read them. Sure, you may have to haul them with you on moving day, but the information you can glean from the articles and ads could help put you ahead of the pack.
- Be patient and don't give up. It's relatively easy to find a job; it's a lot more difficult, however, to find a good job that you like. Do it right and you're likely to get something closer to what you want.
- Remind your working spouse that you need support during the course of your search.

These strategies can be used to help you find work after moving as well.

Your spouse's employer can be a great help during this period. Spousal assistance is a key recruitment and retention issue for many large corporations. The ERC reports that nearly 50 percent of the companies it surveyed offered some kind of employment help for relocating spouses (14 percent for unmarried domestic partners). But don't wait for the company to come to you. It's best to be proactive and seek as much support as possible. Sometimes just a phone call to a company's relocation manager can turn what you may perceive to be an insurmountable problem into something more manageable. Further, this person can help keep you focused and offer a fairly accurate assessment of the local economic market.

Starting Over

Like anyone starting a new job, relocating spouses must be prepared to prove themselves all over again. Relocating spouses must understand that they will need to establish credibility.

It doesn't matter how talented or proficient you may have been in a previous job. Proving yourself is just part of the package of being new. It's human nature for employers to want to put you to the test; people want to know the risk/benefit ratio before they make a wholehearted investment. That seems to go for stocks, mutual funds, and new hires. Taking advantage of the resources at hand and maintaining enthusiasm, however, are about all you should ask of yourself.

As you develop a rapport with the relocation manager, try to assess exactly how much support—financial and otherwise—the company is willing to provide. Inquire, for instance, about "spousal continuation of salary," a quasi-stipend given to help the relocating partner make an easier transition. Tread carefully, however, as you ask about support. If your tone is demanding or you are perceived as too needy, you may not be successful. Saying "please" and "thank you" never goes out of style. Furthermore, it is essential that you acknowledge any help that you do receive. Finally, many companies' partner assistance programs are evolving, so your patience will probably be appreciated.

Taking Your Time

If you're unsure about working or would prefer to become better acquainted with the business community before taking a job—and you have the economic resources—by all means take your time. Researching an area before committing to one job will help you make a sound decision when the time does come to start working.

Some companies arrange for their new hire's spouses to meet with career counselors who can shepherd their clients through a variety of strategies specifically intended to help those who have transferred from another location. Often the assistance will come from third-party providers that offer comprehensive programs designed to ease the transition for the entire family. For example, a career counseling company may customize a program to fit a relocating partner's particular needs. One person may opt for community orientation; another may need help sharpening his or her interviewing skills.

Diana, a relocating spouse with a law degree, sought help from Career Development Services in her efforts to craft what career planners call a "portfolio career," which combines a variety of professional interests. After a series of meetings with her career counselor, she found that a traditional legal career was not the path she wanted to take. Results of a self-assessment exercise amplified her inclination to enter teaching. Today she combines a part-time teaching career with a practice in international law and mediation

Back to School

You may consider going back to school to facilitate your job search. Perhaps you've been thinking about changing directions and seeking a new degree. Or maybe you need to polish your skills in a particular area. Taking classes in a new location is also an excellent way to network and make new friends.

and has more time to spend with her young daughter. "I've been able to create a career that's suited to my lifestyle," says Diana.

Narrowing the Gender Gap

A few years ago, a relocating partner who happened to be a "he" might have been tangling with a cultural taboo. But today, the number of women relocating is on the rise. According to *Runzheimer Reports on Relocation,* an industry newsletter, women make up nearly one-fifth of the total transferee base. In fact, the percentage of women transferees has increased four points from 16 percent in 1993 to 20 percent in 1997. Some experts say that by the year 2000 women will comprise one-third of all transferees.

With our dual-career society, these role reversals are inevitable and, in some measure, are expected to be taken in stride. Still, playing a part you haven't rehearsed isn't easy. If you're a guy who hasn't yet found a job in the new location, you may be asking your wife for grocery money. Is there really any training for that? Likewise, if you're a woman who has left a solid career to follow your mate, accepting a portion of your partner's paycheck may leave you depressed, even humiliated. The truth is, role reversals aren't reserved for one gender anymore.

Seeking Balance

It's easy—enticing even—to become consumed with and by your new job. Change is exhilarating. Meeting challenges with all your might is fulfilling. And if you want to succeed in the workplace, meeting the challenge is also mandatory. To survive, many of us separate the nitty-gritty business of work from other parts of our lives: work, family, work, work, work, and—oh, yeah—family. Unfortunately, it's easy to get stuck, putting on the back burner the very thing you've worked so hard to achieve—a life beyond work, a family life, a home life, a personal life. It's true that some people are opting to commute long distances rather than uproot their families to another location. But even then, commuting time puts a crimp in the dinner hour.

Sometimes, when our family is under the more-than-usual-amount of stress, my husband and I talk about "getting things under control" almost to the exclusion of everything else. Then it hits me that as we're trying to get a grip, our kids' lives are (sort of) rolling merrily along. "This is their life," I say. "These are their days. We can't just put everything on hold while we try to figure things out."

Just because your life is in turmoil or your focus is extremely narrow doesn't mean that the people and the world around you stop to watch. Lives continue. And this continuation is especially critical after a move. Leaving your family behind (both literally and figuratively) can have dire consequences for everyone. Building your life around your work may seem like a requirement. But to do so at the risk of disenfranchising your family may impact your personal happiness in the long term.

Work-life (or work-family) balance is elusive, especially during the course of a major life change. One day, balance is clear and apparent. Everything goes smoothly and everyone is happy—you might even get a full night's sleep. Other days, balance is nonexistent.

Many variables factor into a person's ability to achieve balance. A supportive spouse, well-adjusted children, a truly family-friendly workplace—all can contribute to a smooth transition. But remove one of those elements, and the picture can change dramatically. It's the rare individual who has each piece in place all of the time. Most people I know, working or not, are in constant motion, responding to a cacophony of demands. Balance really becomes something to shoot for rather than an end in and of itself.

In some circumstances, balance is essential. Evenly distributing your efforts into work and family becomes more and more difficult when one side of the axis demands an inordinate amount of your attention. Work—especially new work in a new location—usually wins. Most of the experts interviewed for this book agree that preparation is the best strategy for weathering that part of the transition storm that splits the work-family paradigm. Both partners must recognize that anyone put into a brand-new work situation must not only do the job at hand but establish credibility as well. New employees are constantly being judged and evaluated. Plus, an employee's ability to make smooth transitions varies depending on his or her past experience. One person may just slide right in; another may need more time.

Fighting the Weekend Warrior

Weekends may offer the promise of uninterrupted work time, yet something else is sacrificed—your personal life, your family life. If you must work on the weekends, fight your weekend warrior instincts and offer yourself (and your family) a compromise. Set aside some time for business and leave the rest of the weekend free to connect with the ones who need you, the ones you love.

Even if mobility is a way of life, it's tempting to let balance find its own way into your daily life. But it's not that easy. In order to maximize your (and, hence, your family's) ability to settle in, it's important to make a conscious effort to establish and maintain some semblance of balance.

Unless you first recognize the value of bringing your family with you as you go careening down the professional fast track, it's nearly impossible to value balance and how it can help make your days easier. Balance means accepting the fact that unstructured family time is as important as team-building in your new job. Balance means taking time to ask how your spouse's or partner's day has gone, as well as sitting down with your supervisor to assess the progress of a new product launch. Balance means taking a step back when you're approaching the breaking point. For many people, balance requires a commitment to some higher being or simply a spiritual awareness. If this works for you, by all means incorporate it into your life.

Work-life scales are fickle. What's a priority one day is back-burnered the next. What is seemingly too far out in the future to even think about moves center stage in a matter of minutes. Like change, balance is ephemeral. Yet some things should remain steady: Your family's need to stay intact; your support of a spouse who may have given up a good job to relocate; your steadfast presence in your child's life.

A worker's productivity can be adversely affected by home life stresses. Yet before the stress hits the workplace, it takes a psychically draining detour to home base. Research conducted by the Families and Work Institute shows that people stressed by work-family issues are three times more likely to express their stress at home. Most workers are pretty good at containing their stress at work and generally know the risks associated with taking their frustrations out on fellow workers or their supervisors. But living the stress at home will inevitably makes its way to the workplace, where the employee will simply not be working at full throttle.

Finding Balance

It is possible to balance your act—most of the time. Here are some strategies to help you get there:

- Break the habit of using your office to escape from home stresses. Approach the issues at home with honesty, an open mind, and a willingness to change.
- Know what's important and act accordingly. Level with your employer and say, "Here's what's important to me."
- Never stop examining how your work life mixes with your personal life.
- Ask yourself the tough questions like "Am I spending enough time at home?" "Do I really need to be at my job 14 hours a day, five days a week?" "What does my spouse need?" "Am I taking advantage of the support I'm getting at work?" "Are my employer's values congruent with my own?"
- Try to accurately gauge your company's family-friendly policies, and do what you can to meet your company half-way as you try to balance work and home life.
- Don't underestimate the power of "quantity" time versus "quality" time; just hanging out and "doing nothing" with your family goes a long way toward cementing familial relationships.
- Share your work life with your family. Entrust them with your ups and downs.
- Do something for yourself beyond work, even beyond family. Find a passion that will help you connect to your new surroundings or duplicate an activity or hobby that you enjoyed in your previous location.

Psychologists recommend that the person who precipitates a move work with his or her family to develop a set of realistic expectations of what life is going to look like during the transition. It's important, for example, to admit up front just how hard it is. Starting a new job in a new location is a huge, emotionally exhausting challenge. Yet rather than bemoan this fact, people in this position have a responsibility to sit down with their families and take some time to get centered. They need to shut the phone off, explore communications, and talk about what's happening, good and bad.

Support for Your Soulmate

As you open up and talk, it's equally important to listen to what's *not* being said. Your relocating partner probably doesn't want to "rain on your parade." So while your mate may not seem disheartened by the move, he or she may harbor feelings of resentment, but may be unable or unwilling to allow those sentiments to surface. Open up the lines of communication by doing the following:

- Encourage your partner to express his or her feelings, but be prepared for some honest discussion.
- Assure your partner that it's okay to be dissatisfied and unhappy.
- Tell your partner (more than once) that you appreciate the sacrifice that's been made.
- Ask your employer for spousal/partner assistance. More companies are recognizing the bottom line value of helping star employees. Remember, it never—well, usually never—hurts to ask. And what's not spelled out in a policy may be agreed upon during a face-to-face meeting.

❖

Work/Life:
A Precarious Balance at Best

After we moved to the Northeast, my husband took three weeks off before officially starting work. In some ways, I think those weeks were even more critical for me than they were for him. The time allowed him to learn what functioned in the house and what needed some attention. It also gave him a chance to explore the area and meet new neighbors, particularly the under-three crowd that quickly became a focal point for our daughter.

For me, it meant not being left alone as soon as the moving truck rolled out of the neighborhood. His temporary all-day presence also gave me a chance to venture out on my own without scrambling for a baby-sitter. For all of us, it was a golden opportunity to be together at a very fragile moment. While he looked forward to a new start, I looked ahead with trepidation and a little indigestion. Yet our reliance on one another enabled us to see the future through a shared lens.

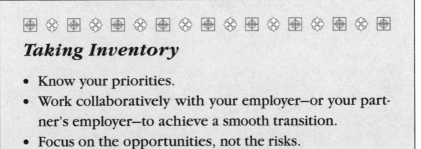

Taking Inventory

- Know your priorities.
- Work collaboratively with your employer—or your partner's employer—to achieve a smooth transition.
- Focus on the opportunities, not the risks.
- Communicate with your family.
- Give yourself time.

Chapter 3

Relocating Spouses and Partners: A Package Deal?

The course of true love never did run smooth.

—William Shakespeare, *A Midsummer Night's Dream*

For the movers who are starting new jobs, relocating can be exhilarating. For many workers, relocating is about promotions, professional advancement and recognition, or the opportunity to start a dream career. But for the accompanying spouse or partner the mere thought of relocating can touch off an emotional tremor that can turn a life upside down.

This chapter focuses on how relocating partners can overcome the obstacles presented by a move and seek out opportunities that will make the move a more enriching experience. Further, the chapter is directed toward the relocating partner, but to truly make the tips work, you've got to tackle the situation as a couple. Your relationship–your partnership–must take center stage. It's got to be the glue–the cement, really–that keeps your lives somewhat whole. So even if your goal is to reclaim a portion of your life that may be diminished due to the move, the quality of your partner's life should be an integral part of your strategy. And your partner's participation in helping you achieve that goal is absolutely essential. You might even try reading this chapter together. Think of it as good medicine for the health of your relationship.

Help from Outside

Not too long ago, American corporations began to recognize that in order to attract and retain the best and brightest, they had to have relocation policies that reflected the needs of the talent they were courting as well as of their partners and families. Today, many relocation packages take these needs into account.

Relocation experts agree that companies must be more flexible and innovative so that their collective bottom lines don't bottom out. All of this is good news for relocating partners. Even if your partner's employer doesn't have a formal policy in place, it's not unusual for companies to improvise if it becomes necessary. In fact, if you haven't been offered some kind of assistance from your partner's employer, take a proactive stance and simply inquire about any help they may be able to offer. If you want something badly enough—and make it known—everyone around you might very well conspire to help you get what you're after.

Many companies offer relocating partners premove counseling via telephone. A career counselor or relocation manager can help you get a jump-start on the local labor market in your new city. This is a great boon for partners who want as little disruption in their careers as necessary and relieves some of the pressure and anxiety people feel when they don't know what's ahead. A counselor also can offer perspective in terms of any options that may be available.

Larger companies typically offer some kind of program designed to ease a partner's transition. Some firms, however, do not offer assistance to unmarried partners, though as their relocation policies evolve, "spousal" assistance may be expanded to include help for partners regardless of gender. Partner reemployment and lost-wage compensation are two options you can ask for. If you have children, inquire about any help the company is willing to provide for finding child care or school assistance for your older kids. (For help on finding work in your new location, see Chapter 2.)

Hearing the stories of other relocating partners is another way to obtain reassurance. Ask the relocation manager at your partner's company for the names of other relocated partners with whom you might connect. Meeting other like-minded people is a great way to make contacts as well. Many relocating partners form lasting alliances and can help one another through the initial stages of a move. A special compatibility and a shared language can facilitate such relationships.

Self-Help

Here are four things you should do as soon as you have a dial tone on your phone line:

1. *Call old friends and colleagues to say hi.* Don't wait to send out change-of-address-cards to give them vital information they'll need to stay in touch.
2. *Join professional or philanthropic organizations and volunteer on a few committees.* Your involvement will help you establish your credibility in the community and provide a good resource for what's happening around town.
3. *Invite your neighbors over for an impromptu get-together.* Serve some light refreshments and encourage them to tell you about the new neighborhood. (If you have children, ask for baby-sitter recommendations, too.)
4. *Sign up for an exercise class at a local health club, YMCA, YWCA, JCC, or other athletic facility.* It'll be good for your mind, body, and spirit and help you meet more people in the community.

Hearing versus Listening

Knowing you've been heard is a soothing tonic for any relationship. This is particularly true if you're angry or resentful. If you are resentful of the move, let your partner know. Remember, however, that resenting the move is different from resenting your partner. Your communications should reflect this. If not, you may alienate your partner, who may subsequently find it difficult to validate your feelings.

Tokens for the Psychic Tollbooth

For the accompanying partner, relocating may be disruptive, disorienting, and even a little depressing. So what's the upside? Actually, the opportunities for you are not terribly different from those of your mate. Certainly relocating to a new land, whether it's the next town over or a state you've seen only on a map, means change. Change can be good, very good. If you can organize your new life in a way that embraces change, you may be surprised at how successful and happy you can become.

Whether you're a he or a she, relocating can put a major strain on even the closest relationships. Maybe you've been yanked from a job you found fulfilling. Or perhaps you were just getting used to the last location. Quite possibly you've left the only community you've ever known, not to mention your entire family. Or maybe this move is exactly what you've been waiting for. The circumstances of relocating are as varied as the people who fuel this industry in the first place. But the emotions are yours and must never be minimized. Even if this particular move has positive outcomes—a bigger household salary, a bigger home, a better climate—it may still be a wrenching experience that must be tended to and taken care of.

Naturally, you'll need "tokens" for the psychic tollgate. That's right—some kind of currency that will help you navigate the path toward settling in and making a new place for yourself. Effective communication methods, destressors, self-comforting activities (the kind that build your self-esteem and reenergize you) are just a few of the items you'll need to get through the barriers you may encounter.

You'll also need information. Maybe you'll have to learn how to access that information. Maybe you'll find yourself tired of asking people questions. You might even consider giving up, throwing in the towel, calling it quits. That's very tempting, but it will net you nothing: No new friends, no new activities, no new favorite bakeries. And that would be a big loss.

The point here is to scoop up tokens—your emotional currency—and spend them on whatever you need in order to maintain your self-esteem and a solid collaborative relationship with your partner.

Anchors and Charms

If you're in the midst of a move or even in the process of settling in, feeling anchored may seem illusive, an impossibility. Yet just because your feet aren't firmly planted doesn't mean you're without the security that will eventually provide a strong base. If you feel as though you're drifting far from shore, consider introducing (or welcoming back) anchoring rituals. Anchoring rituals don't need to be left behind in your old location. It is a concept that you can carry with you all over the world.

Here are a few anchoring rituals you and your partner might consider:

- Plan for regularly scheduled "date nights." If you have children, schedule the sitter ahead of time to turn it into a real routine.
- Search out a new favorite breakfast spot (or coffee shop, or restaurant) and make it "yours."
- Find a new mutual interest in your new location.

- Schedule a monthly lunch with your mate.
- Invite a new couple to dinner once a month to expand your base of friends and acquaintances.
- Select a point of interest—a park, museum, or historic district—each month that you'll both scout out together.

If these don't send you, create your own anchoring rituals. Jot them down and post them on a bulletin board that you both can see on a daily basis. Remember: The idea is to do something that reinforces your commitment to each other.

Don't Be Afraid to Ask

Your work—your life—should not be an afterthought. However, most moves are precipitated by the career of one, not two. Renegotiating whose career is more important in the midst of a move is not only exhausting but really is not very useful either. Practicing effective communications, on the other hand, is useful and can prevent some conflicts from escalating to unmanageable levels.

At the Center for Marital and Family Studies at the University of Denver, researchers have determined that the method couples use to handle conflicts and disagreements predicts with 93 percent accuracy which folks will split up and divorce and which will remain married. That's a fairly startling statistic and one that all couples should pay close attention to.

If you're in the midst of a taxing transition, it's not unusual to allow basic communications channels to get clogged up. You and your partner are simply too busy with all the changes to take time that is normally a part of your daily (or weekly) routine. The irony, however, is that the relationship takes a back seat when it should be a priority.

Try taking the following quiz to find out if your relationship needs some serious attention after relocating. Answer true or false to the following:

My partner spends so much time at the new job that we hardly ever get a chance to catch up on each other's lives.	T F
All my partner ever talks about is the new job. He (She) never asks how I'm doing.	T F
I seem to be doing all the housework. Before we moved, we used to share chores.	T F
Even on the weekends we never seem to have a few minutes with each other.	T F
Our romance and sex life are definitely suffering.	T F
What used to feel like a partnership now seems to be a convenient arrangement.	T F
My partner seems to have completely forgotten that I have career aspirations, too.	T F

Answering true to any, or all, of these statements is certainly not unusual after relocating. But once you've settled in, a steady pattern of true answers may raise a red flag indicating that the move is putting too much strain on your relationship. If this is the case, consider seeking help from a therapist who specializes in counseling couples. Don't let your fear of others "finding out" what's happening prevent you from getting the assistance you need to safeguard your relationship. Communication roadblocks between couples are common, especially during a stressful time. The mistake is to ignore the warning signs. Left unchecked, the roadblocks can lead to other problems.

If you suspect, for instance, that your periodic bouts of sadness are turning into depression or if you are concerned about your partner's emotional well-being, consider seeking professional help. The best place to start is with someone you trust—a new friend, physician, your rabbi, minister, or another member of your place of worship. Spousal assistance is often available through your partner's employer as well. Consider asking a local radio talk-show psychologist or therapist about counseling resources in your new location.

Regardless of where or from whom you receive references, shop around. Counseling, like legal advice or medical treatment, is a service that you should be comfortable with. Don't be afraid of setting up an interview with two or three therapists you're interested in meeting. State your intentions up front—that you're first trying to determine a good fit—and be prepared to pay for their time. Ask each person if he or she specializes in couples or individual therapy. You should also feel free to raise the issues you'll be talking about when formal therapy begins. Try to gauge the therapist's comfort level in talking with you about these issues.

Once you've selected someone to see, don't feel obligated to continue if you don't feel you're being helped or if you feel uncomfortable. This is a match that should work for you, not against you.

If you want your partner to accompany you for counseling, be open and ask for his or her participation. If your partner balks at the idea or simply withdraws and makes no commitment one way or the other, let him or her know that you'd like support but must proceed with the counseling because it is something you need to do for yourself. Try not to view your mate's lack of interest as a closed door. Instead, think of it as a temporary setback that you will overcome in time.

You may also want to seek out others who are experiencing the same feelings. A support group may help alleviate feelings of alienation. It may also serve as an effective stopgap before settling on a therapist. It's quite possible that you might even meet interesting people. Try calling local social services agencies, religious institutions, community centers, and your physician for referrals. If you prefer anonymity and don't need the human touch, visit the World Wide Web. Online services also include a variety of forums (interest groups) that you may tap into.

Expect the Expected

Forget about the unexpected. You have no control over those things anyway. What you can control—or at least prepare for—are circumstances that are likely to occur after relocating. Take your partner's new job, for instance. You probably should expect (and plan for) a period during which your partner will be completely absorbed with and immersed in his or her new position. It may last three months; it may last longer. If you know this ahead of time, you are more likely to take care of your own needs early on. This, in turn, will compress the adjustment period. Just remember, it's a temporary, but necessary, stage in the relocating process.

Stating the Emotions and Emotional States

When life throws spears your way (like when you're relocating), communicating with your partner in a rational and calm manner can become a little difficult. You might feel as if the two of you are spiraling downward at a rate that's beyond your control. It almost becomes easier to dodge the spears and forfeit your feelings to a noncommunicative oblivion.

Instead of ducking when one of these destructive weapons is hurled in your direction, reach up and grab one. Examine it, strip it of its harmful power, and retire it to where it belongs— far away from your heart, mind, and soul. It's not easy at first, but with practice you will become a natural. Here are some ways to protect you and your partner from the corrosive effects of poor communication:

- Express any frustrations in a noncritical, unthreatening manner.
- Share your partner's enthusiasm for his or her new job.

Hazardous Work Sites and Other Explosive Environments

A woman I know wanted desperately to champion her husband's new job and subsequent move. Yet her feelings of resentment and sadness over leaving her family prevented her from truly siding with his newfound success. It was no surprise then that after several weeks in the new house she erupted with volcanic force, yelling, "I am so mad at you for moving us here!" For her, this unscheduled expression of angst and anger helped diffuse a tense situation. For her partner, it clarified some of her frustrations and opened up an opportunity for further, more rational, discussion.

- Give and ask for expressions of appreciation.
- Remind yourself and your partner that the relationship takes precedence over the new job, house, whatever.
- Share your worries and fears before they become unmanageable.
- Be honest about your expectations.
- Schedule "together" time on a regular basis (nightly, weekly).
- Write your feelings in a letter. (You may do this just to help yourself feel better, or you can share it with your mate.)
- Learn how to validate—recognize and respect—one another's feelings.
- Try not to dwell on the sacrifice you've made; look at it as an opportunity.

Lost and Found: Finding Your Place

As the relocating partner, you've probably left behind myriad tangible and intangible possessions. Not only are you exploring brand-new physical and emotional territories, you're likely to be mourning what you held near and dear. Even as you reach out to embrace your new community, you may still be actively maintaining ties with people in your old location. Balancing these two types of relationships is not easy. Nonetheless, it's a normal part of the mourning process. You'll probably find that the more you become involved in your new environment, the less you will be bound to the people and places you left behind.

Lonely or Independent?

One of the most painful aspects of moving is the utter loneliness and despair that can enshroud you. After we moved, my husband took three weeks off to help us get settled, spend some time with the family, and establish his own bearings. Having him around so much helped me forget about my anxieties. Unfortunately, once he started his new job, I was starkly reminded of my somewhat independent and directionless future.

I vividly recall a lunchtime visit with my daughter to a nearby fast-food restaurant. All the patrons seemed to be like me: Mothers snitching french fries from their noisy little charges. On that particular day, however, I noticed that many there seemed fed up. No one looked happy. People were shouting at their children, who were crying, which naturally incited their mothers to keep screaming, and so on. I leaned over to my daughter and quietly said, "We will never do this again."

It was many, many months before I went back. But even more important than my personal boycott was my resolve to keep myself out of situations that brought me down. From that moment on I would seek opportunities that would raise my spirits and help me adopt the new community as my own.

I still experienced times of immense loneliness, but more and more I became exhilarated by my newfound independence. Yet I noticed that, while my husband and I were probably spending the same amount of time together that we had in the past, it seemed as if we saw each other less. Before relocating, I had filled up my days with a full-time job and the care of our daughter. Now my days were filled up with too much of me. My husband was really the only other adult figure in my life, and I began to miss him terribly.

I won't tell you the number of times I used to call his office. But I will tell you that I started to think about what I could do to fill some of my time and contain the emptiness that periodically crept in and out of my consciousness. One of the first things I did was to begin some volunteer work. First, I put in some time at a local hospice. After that, I volunteered at the local Ronald McDonald House. Both experiences gave me a chance to meet new people, do something useful, and learn about the goodwill in my new community.

If you're not working full-time, think about what you could do that you would enjoy and that would help you become embedded in your community. Most areas have a gazillion opportunities for volunteer work. But just as you would do in seeking "real" work, try to seek out situations that seem appealing. Maybe you've always wondered about becoming involved in broadcasting. A call to your local public radio or television station could land you a volunteer position that could enrich your new life tenfold. Perhaps you've put that art class on hold until the time was "right." If you're an avid reader, a book group might be the thing for you. Most libraries, even some bookstores, can direct you to people with similar goals.

Overcoming Self-Defeating Behaviors

Unfortunately, relocating is fertile ground for giving in to self-defeating behaviors. Adjusting to a new community is hard, exhausting work. It's also risky, which makes the process even less appealing. If you're prone to sabotaging your own success, take the following precautions:

- Do whatever is necessary to keep your self-esteem at its highest.
- Choose activities and set goals that are your own, not someone else's.

- Try not to worry about what others think of you.
- If a new activity begins to lose its appeal, replace it with something else and move on. Letting go of losing propositions doesn't make you a quitter; it just means you're selective and you want what's right for you.
- Resist the temptation to procrastinate. Good opportunities are ephemeral; catch them when you can.
- Recognize your human frailties and accept your mistakes. A sense of humor will make this even easier.
- Identify and try to minimize stress that can feed into self-defeating behaviors.

If you quit a job to relocate with your partner, be patient with yourself as you settle into your new routine. Let's say before the move you put in ten-hour days and worked at a ridiculous pace. The break from your old routine may be a welcomed one. Yet you may still pine for the excitement, involvement, control, and any other elements that comprised your own professional life. Unless you tend to these feelings, your self-esteem may begin to waver.

If it becomes unbearable to stay home every day, for instance, then schedule an activity that will take you out of your house and into the community. It might just be treating yourself to a quiet cup of coffee every Tuesday morning, or visiting the library every Thursday afternoon. What's important here is that you create a system for sending and receiving care packages for your heart and soul—something to regenerate your spirit.

By the same token, resist the temptation to do things that may work for one newcomer but not for you. If you have kids, for instance, but get squeamish at the idea of play groups, come up with a good substitute like individual play dates or library story hours. On the other hand, try to strike a balance between activities that turn you off and those that you simply aren't sure of. If you say no to everything, you're likely to get deeper and deeper into your own space. Say yes to some and maybe you'll find something that will change your life in wonderful ways.

Act "As If"

Soon after we moved into our new home, I was visited by our local Welcome Wagon® representative. Left with a pile of coupons after she had gone, I reconsidered my "I'm not a joiner" stance and called a number to RSVP for the upcoming meeting. At the meeting, I simply acted as if I knew exactly what I was doing and what I wanted. I think most of the other people there did the same thing. I only stayed with the group for a little over a year, but I reaped an important reward: a friend with whom I am still close.

Remember, too, that everyone approaches adversity in different ways and at different rates. One relocated partner may move at breakneck speed to adjust and feel at home. You, on the other hand, may be quite comfortable to take life at a slower pace. That's okay. And if you change gears midway through the adjustment process, that's okay, too.

In Harmony

In relationships where one partner works or works more than the other, no one issue seems to raise more frustration than the amount of time that partner devotes to home life. The frustration often leads to stress, which then leads to anger. For the relocated partner, the frustration, mixed with the normal resentment that accompanies a move, can set off an electrical surge that may not only burn the partner but can scorch the entire relationship as well.

Thomas Jefferson once said that when you're angry, count to ten before you speak; when you're really angry count to 100. Yet counting won't change whatever is frustrating you. But talking to your partner might. Just keep in mind that the *way* you talk will certainly have a direct impact on your success.

If you believe that your partner is neglecting certain areas of your lives, gently remind him or her that despite the move, you still depend on his or her participation in domestic matters. Try saying, "I understand that you want to focus on your new job, but I'm feeling a little overwhelmed by all the day-to-day responsibilities. I could really use your help."

It's true that a working partner—especially one who's just started a new position—is usually investing in the family's financial well-being. But there's more to being a good provider than regularly depositing money into the checking account. Consider these additional areas that could benefit by everyone's participation:

- *Domestic chores.* This may range from laundry, to grocery shopping, to taking suits to the dry cleaners.
- *Time (quality and quantity).* Just being around in the midst of normal domestic chaos can enhance the equilibrium of your relationship.
- *Time management (planning).* This can be a particularly annoying sore spot for the chief planner, since he or she may be unaware of something you've scheduled (family outings, vacations, parties, kids' activities, etc.) or would like to schedule. And what if there is no chief planner? Then whose job is it? It's best to share this key responsibility. It'll keep your family's future on track and help everyone avoid unnecessary discord.

Identity Run Amok

My friends used to marvel over the fact that my husband and I never had a joint checking account—not until we moved, that is. I had stopped working and simply had no money coming in. I gasped when the box of checks arrived in the mail. Both of our names appeared on the checks, since we opted for a reduced administrative fee. "That's it!" I thought. "I've got to get a job." My husband assured me that the account was mine, and to this day it

---

Clueless or Just Tunnel Vision?

If your working partner seems unaware of or not interested in your frustrations (or, in some cases, bottled-up rage), don't despair. What may seem like positively clueless behavior may simply be your partner's obsessive though necessary drive to achieve in his or her new job. New workers are almost always at a disadvantage compared with their more tenured colleagues. There's so much to catch up on and find out about. It's exhausting, which may leave your partner too tired to do anything else, much less think about what you may be going through. So before you accuse your beloved of being insensitive, try to imagine the pressures of being the new kid on the business block. And then rationally talk about your concerns.

---

is; he has never signed one of those checks. But at the time, it felt like a concession.

Trading places doesn't have to put you in a tailspin. My friend Jeff spent a few years in Japan, where his wife was a captain in the U.S. Air Force. Most people assumed he was the officer, not his wife. They'd salute Jeff and generally treat *him* like the officer. That attitude seems to be changing, however, as more and more women with civilian partners are joining the military.

Many men who relocate for their partner's careers do so out of a reciprocal desire to please—an integral piece of the marriage pact. Two men I know followed their wives because they knew the moves would make their mates happy. Frank and Rae, who moved from the Northeast to the Southwest, had talked about moving for a few years before actually investigating job opportunities elsewhere. "We'd already decided that Rae would be the one more likely to garner a higher salary, even though jobs in her expertise were limited," explains Frank. "For me, on the other hand, jobs were more prevalent, though at a lower pay scale." It made sense for this couple to pool their needs so that they could make a move that satisfied all their requirements.

Another male relocating partner left a lucrative position in sales to follow his wife who had received a promotion at a pharmaceutical company. To get a job in the new location, John had to take a pay cut. "You have to get beyond the bruised ego that may occur when you take a cut in pay," he says.

For John and his wife, and other couples as well, the circumstances that lead up to a move can have as much to do with their ultimate decision as the opportunity itself. "Peggy stayed home for years to raise our children. Once they were grown, she wanted to try something new," John says. "Now it's my turn to sacrifice."

Don't Forget to Dance

After my husband and I relocated, we endured (off and on) an intense struggle that seemed positively menacing. Our home life was not always harmonious. Quite frankly, what I hoped would be a refuge often felt more like domestic purgatory.

Yet like a ferocious rainstorm that begins and ends in a matter of minutes, our conflicts helped to clear the air, making our spirits more sturdy, our love more solid. At one point, early on in our new home, I asked my husband to dance. He will probably never admit it or will claim he doesn't remember. But we danced. Like other firsts—our first steaks on the grill, our first night of entertaining—this dance symbolically affirmed and reminded me of my commitment to a man I trust, respect, and cherish. With his support and love, I think I'd relocate to the moon.

❈ ❖ ❈ ❖ ❈ ❖ ❈ ❖ ❈ ❖ ❈ ❖ ❈ ❖ ❈ ❖ ❈

Taking Inventory

- Inquire (or ask your partner to inquire) about possible assistance available from your partner's employer.
- Take care of yourself.
- Don't be afraid to ask for help.
- Seek out other relocating partners who can offer friendship and support.
- Communicate with your partner using noncritical and nonthreatening language.

Chapter 4

"Who Will Sit Next to Me at Lunch?" A Child's Point of View

A mother [father] understands what a child does not say.

—Jewish proverb

$\mathcal{I}$f moving to a new location rattles your nerves, imagine its effects on a child. Even if the move means a better job and a bigger house for you, a child may experience a tremendous sense of loss. And regardless of how commonplace relocating has become, moving is still a big deal for kids.

This chapter focuses on ways in which you can ease your child's transition from one home to the next. The assorted tips and strategies in this chapter will help you be the best guide you can be. You'll also learn that change is never easy and that your instincts are the best barometer for knowing what's best for your child.

Easing Your Child's Stress and Your Own

Moving puts several demands on children. The most difficult to deal with is leaving all that is familiar—friends, family, and surroundings. Anxiety, uncertainty, a sense of loss, and loneliness are common emotions that can occur before, during, and after a move. Plus, unlike adults, children (especially young children) don't have the benefit of past experience to reassure them that feelings and memories move with them wherever they go. Following are some tips to ease the initial transition from old to new:

- Encourage your children to talk about their feelings.
- Listen to what they say and reassure them that you understand.
- Acknowledge their feelings of tangible and intangible loss.
- Don't forsake your own feelings completely, but do temper your moods to enhance your children's feelings of security.
- Remind your children that home truly is where the heart is— family values, traditions, and goals stay the same no matter where you live.
- Be enthusiastic about the new location, but understand your children's need to take things at their own pace—which may be different than yours.

Psychologists agree that the major factor impacting a child's adjustment to moving is the mental health of the parents. If you're under stress, then your child is at risk as well.

Indeed, if you're concerned about how your child is handling the stress of moving, ask yourself how you're doing. If you're down, your child is likely to be blue as well.

Kids tend to follow the behavior and attitudes of their parents. So after a move it's critical for parents to project a positive, hopeful outlook on their new surroundings. Getting out of the house, meeting others, and inviting people over sets a good example and

Become a Joiner

Kids often take cues from their parents. Complement your positive attitude about moving by becoming a joiner. Hook up with your local Welcome Wagon® or join the PTA at your child's new school. (I counted no fewer than 33 PTA committees at my daughter's school.) And if you have the time, volunteer in your child's classroom. Becoming a joiner will help you do the following:

- Make your child feel more secure as you find your own place in the new community.
- Make you feel connected to your new environment.
- Open doors for your child to meet new people and make new friends.
- Teach your child the value of community involvement.
- Demonstrate to others that you're capable of embracing something new.

show kids the benefits of taking the initiative. Remember, though, don't promise that the new place will be a bed of roses. If your child does have a negative experience, you'll lose credibility and your child will lose confidence in your word.

Parents should not wait for or rely on their children, particularly very young kids, to arrange invitations and play dates. It can be extremely difficult for children—adults, too—to break into already formed circles of friendship. Helping your child facilitate friendships will allow your child deal more effectively with separation and attachment issues. Your assistance also will provide a gentle reminder that your child is not alone.

Most children, particularly those ages nine and up, want desperately to fit in. Some kids—maybe yours—may come into a new environment with a different style than their new peers. They want to know the language and ultimately want to be accepted. The more sensitive you are to this issue, the more likely you are to help your child adjust.

Depending on your child's personality, you may be inclined to do things that enhance his or her sense of belonging. Initially, that may mean conforming to the status quo—at first, that is. Helping your child become accepted will hasten the adjustment process; focus on individualism later down the road.

That is not to say that parents should discourage their children from being themselves. It's a good life lesson no matter what age to encourage children to let people see who they really are— within limits, of course.

For example, soon after (or before) a move, your children may be very angry. Acknowledging their feelings is essential; tolerating unacceptable behavior, however, is not necessary. Try to resist the temptation to give in on everything and, instead, maintain your expectations. Kids need boundaries, especially during the fragile period that precedes and follows a move.

"Is There Any Mail for Me?"

Sometimes just getting something—anything—in the mail can perk up a child's spirits. Receiving mail can help give a child a sense of belonging. Subscribing to a magazine in your child's name will provide a steady arrival of mail exclusively for him or her. Check out the Resources section at the end of this book for a list of kid-friendly publications or visit your local library for these and other periodicals devoted to your child's personal hobbies and interests. For best results, read the magazine together.

Preaddressed postcards given to old friends before the move also can serve as a steady supply of mail in the new place. You can also send something yourself. Time it right and your children will be delighted to get a message from Mom or Dad soon after move-in day.

One of the best ways to help children adjust to a move is to simply listen and be available. This is one of those times when you should have a heightened sense of what your children are saying, what they're *not* saying, and how they are behaving. Don't be surprised if your children don their own pairs of rose-colored glasses and rewrite a little history. What might have bothered them before—mean classmates, no one to play with in the neighborhood—may not look so bad compared with what they don't know about the new location.

Safe at Home

With all the chaos whirling around a family in the midst of a move, it is easy to neglect those things we ordinarily take for granted. Like water. Pediatricians and the U.S. Consumer Product Safety Commission recommend that you turn the thermostat on your hot water heater to 120°F. You should also call your local water authority to determine the fluoride content in your tap water. (Babies don't need extra fluoride drops if they are drinking fluoridated tap water.)

The H$_2$O You Know

Tonie Lindenberger, director of relocation services for United Van Lines, suggests that movers transport a few jugs of tap water from the old location to the new. "A lot of kids experience upset stomachs after drinking water in their new homes," she says. "Having water from the old location in the first few days can help kids and their tummies become more acclimated to the drinking water in their new home."

Other perils, like an open, unscreened window, a jar of turpentine, even unexplored stairways, should be eliminated from small children's paths. Moving and the days that follow can be a very dangerous period in a young child's life. Children who move from an apartment to a house with stairs are at particular risk and should be watched carefully in the early days. And don't forget to get those gates up immediately.

Though a lead paint disclosure is usually part of the closing on the purchase of a home, be wary of any chipping paint or plaster. Lead poisoning can occur if it is ingested, which can later affect intelligence and development. If you suspect that your home contains lead paint, talk to your pediatrician about testing and prevention. Take the following precautions as well:

- Look up the number of your local poison control center and post the telephone number in a prominent area of your home—usually near a phone in the kitchen.
- Cover unused electrical sockets with plastic plugs.
- Place new batteries in existing smoke detectors (and install any additional detectors that may be necessary). Then designate move-in day as your change-the-batteries anniversary.
- Add a fire extinguisher to your arsenal (but be sure to read the instructions so that you'll know how to operate it in the event of a fire).
- If they are capable, have your children learn your new address and home and work numbers. Role-playing during the first few months makes this exercise fun.

New Home Medicine Chest

Every home should have one. No one likes sickness or injuries, but you can react more quickly if you're prepared. Stock the following basics for your new home medicine chest:

- A thermometer or two that you can read easily and quickly
- Antihistamine (liquid or tablets) to treat bee stings, allergic reactions, and itching from chicken pox

- Oral electrolyte solution or powder for maintaining hydration for kids who have diarrhea or are vomiting
- Acetaminophen to help reduce fever and aches and pains (This is available in many forms: infant drops, tablets, and elixir. Make sure you purchase the right concentration for your child's age.)
- Skin creams (petroleum jelly for dry skin, Polysporin for minor skin infections, hydrocortisone cream for itchy rashes)
- First-aid kit (bandages, sterile gauze pads and surgical tape, Ace bandage, ice pack—a package of frozen vegetables will work in a pinch, too)

Remember to consult your pediatrician if you have any questions and add to your arsenal any items to accommodate special medical needs (i.e., Epi-pen kit for allergic reactions to bee stings, inhalers or steroids for asthma sufferers). Also, be sure to dispense these products with your pediatrician's approval.

A Doctor in the House

How do you find a pediatrician? If you are lucky enough to have family in your new location, by all means inquire about the doctor they use. Otherwise you'll need to rely on the opinions of new friends, neighbors, and colleagues. Some areas have medical societies that will provide lists of practicing physicians. Hospitals provide referral services as well. But if you can stick with word-of-mouth recommendations, you are more likely to find what you need. Remember, though, popular, well-liked pediatricians must sometimes close their doors to new patients. So cast a wide net when you begin your research.

Before launching your search, arrange to have your child's medical records available. And take some time to review your family's health insurance coverage. Some doctors may not participate in your HMO, for example.

✿

Before the Fact

The tips here are intended to help you find a pediatrician after you have moved. If you happen to be reading this prior to making the trip, here's one piece of advice that could prevent a major headache: If you're moving before the school year begins, arrange for a physical before you move. Getting all the necessary vaccines and health care prior to moving will give you the luxury of finding a pediatrician at your own pace. Otherwise, you might be caught in a time crunch scrambling to find someone in your new community who has an opening to conduct a school physical. The practice may accommodate your immediate need but may not necessarily be the right one for your family.

Once you collect a few names, arrange a meeting with each person so you can determine if there is a fit among your family, the practice, and the physician. More important than the certificates hanging on the examination room's walls is the feeling you get from each office you visit and pediatrician you talk with (though training at and affiliation with a good hospital is important). In addition to learning about the physician's credentials and training, try to get a feel for the doctor's approachability. No one likes to be intimidated, especially a worried parent tending a sick child. Find out about night and weekend coverage. Does the office encourage parents to call after hours? What about Saturday visits?

A pediatrician often becomes a central figure in a family's life and should, therefore, be receptive to and encourage a partnership with the family. If your child has any special needs, be sure to bring that up when you meet with prospective pediatricians. Take note of their reactions to your concerns. Are they sincere?

Will they give you the time necessary to review particular issues that may arise over the years?

Further, your pediatrician should be someone with whom you are comfortable and should have good communications skills. Try to select someone who will foster an open and honest relationship—a relationship that will maximize the physical, emotional, psychological, and social well-being of your child.

Use the same criteria to find a pediatric dentist. Look for a dental practice that has a light and fun atmosphere, with plenty of toys and other distractions that will help minimize any fear or uncertainty. Providing a safe haven during a dental exam can significantly improve a child's perception of a new dental experience.

Business as Usual (Sort of)

Stability and consistency are at the heart of a child's healthy development. But even in the best of times—when moving is not a factor, for instance—we overlook this basic tenet of parenting. Some things are easier to control than others. For example, taking your child's artwork from the old refrigerator and putting it on the new fridge is easy, and it lets your child know that some things do, indeed, stay the same.

On the other hand, regressive behavior is a little more difficult to manage. Temper tantrums may intensify after moving, sleep may be disrupted, and your potty-trained toddler may take three giant steps backward.

Take heart. After a period of adjustment, children generally fall back into their normal routines. Nonetheless, don't let up on conditioning maneuvers after moving. Reestablish the mechanism of conditioning with firm kindness.

It is easy to fall into bad habits, especially when put under stress. But instead of allowing healthy behavior to fall by the wayside, concentrate on exercise that is appealing, activities that bring out the best in everyone, relaxation (when you can fit it in), and, of course, healthy nutrition.

To minimize any after-move tension, put your stress management techniques into high gear. Stay involved in life and avoid dwelling solely on the move. Place yourself in the role of an usher. That is, try to lead the way toward discovering what lies ahead.

Change puts tremendous demands on our psyches. Yet sometimes, while we're nursing the state of our emotional well-being, particularly during a change in our lives, our physical needs—exercise, diet, sleep—are forgotten. As parents, it's our job to monitor diet and nutrition and make sure that all members of the family are getting plenty of relaxation.

Maintaining involvement with relatives (even if it's just via telephone, snail mail, or e-mail), religious organizations, athletic activities, and socializing can help minimize the negative effects that change can have on a family.

Probably most important for young children after a move is your dependable presence. That is not to say that you must never leave your child's sight. Learning that you will safely return after each absence helps instill coping mechanisms that in turn will ease the whole transition phase.

Just Say Fun

In my house, asking children if they want to have fun is almost equivalent to offering candy for breakfast. Just saying the word evokes enough excitement and joyful anticipation to get things started. Sometimes my kids like to review and preview their days in measurements of fun.

"What was fun about today?" they'll ask at bedtime as I'm saying goodnight and "What will be fun about tomorrow?"

Simply speaking, fun goes a long way with children. Fun is also a soothing antidote for combating stress. Here are some fun after-moving-in activities that will help quicken the pulse of your child:

- Take a bucket of colored chalk out to the driveway or sidewalk and go to town to create artistic neighborhood graffiti. (This will attract other kids like moths to your outdoor light!)
- Plant a perennial garden so your child has something to look forward to each year.
- For your young teen, invite a new friend to a sleepover. Provide plenty of food, videos, and privacy. Creating a welcoming environment for new friends goes a long way toward setting a positive tone.
- Surprise your child with homemade coupons. Create your own vouchers that especially appeal to kids and then hide them around the house. A special toy, lunch at a favorite new restaurant, a manicure in your very own, private nail salon—anything that will provide a little lift. Don't plant the coupons all at once, however; your child may turn out to be quite the explorer and discover all of them on one journey.
- If it is summer, construct a lemonade stand—a traditional gathering place for meeting new people.
- Have a recycling party for all the items you couldn't part with but cannot wait to get rid of now that you have arrived at your destination. Consider donating old linens, toys, and games to local homeless shelters, children's hospitals, or schools. This is a great way to teach your kids the value of giving back to the community that serves them.
- If you're snowbound, get the sleds out and explore any nearby hills. Pack a thermos of hot chocolate, and you'll really win points. Even if you haven't unpacked the sleds or they're still on the list of "need to buy," take a walk and enjoy the universal beauty of a snowfall. And don't forget the marshmallows!
- Any packing boxes left over from the move? Take the really big boxes, and, with some markers, paint, and any other materials create houses, stores, and whatever else is residing in your child's imagination.

A Symbol of Security

One of the best ways to help your children become personally connected to their new surroundings is to share the environment and encourage a sense of steward-ship. Steve Bennett, author of *365 TV-Free Activities You Can Do with Your Child,* suggests that kids adopt trees. Adopting a nearby tree after moving can give your children a real sense of security and belonging.

Your yard, a park, or any public place will do. Bark rubbings, collecting leaves, and measuring the trunk will help your children and the tree become better acquainted. Your children can visit the tree year after year and even return as an adult. After all, what could be more solid and enduring than a tree?

Go Ahead, Be a Tourist

Remember the T-shirt that read, "I'm not a tourist. I live here"? Well, in some cases, outfitting yourself in tourist gear can reap great rewards. Our impulse to observe and document our surroundings is human nature. We hold near and dear our scrapbooks, photo albums, and personal journals. You can help your children grow new roots and create a personal history by encouraging them to explore their new hometown.

To get started, secure a large map and as many brochures as you (or your kids) can carry from your visitor's center or chamber of commerce. Take a trip, with kids in tow, around town and note special places—pizza joints, playgrounds, the library, ice cream parlors, video rental stores, toy stores, and museums. Once you are back home, mark the kid-friendly locations with bright stickers. Then put the map where it can be seen and used.

School Days

Whether you've moved in the middle of the summer or during the school year, changing schools can be a major source of discomfort for children at any age. Teens are especially vulnerable at this time and should get as much support from you as possible.

"School is a child's career," says Priscilla Toomey, president of MovePower, Inc., a Riverside, Connecticut–based relocation assistance firm. "Even if you only move a short distance, a change of schools turns the child's world upside down."

The Midyear Move

Most families prefer to move just after the school year has ended or before it is about to start. If you do have the option, consider relocating in the middle of the school year when a new face can pull youngsters out of the winter doldrums and put your child in the spotlight. In the summer, you risk moving into a neighborhood whose kids are nowhere to be found. They are ensconced in summer camp, on vacation, or off visiting relatives.

Who is not intimidated by a strange and large group of people that seems to know exactly what is happening? For the new kid in school, jolly voices and peals of laughter can seem frightening and even exclusionary. Meet with teachers, principals, counselors, and anyone else likely to have contact with your children before school begins. It's important for parents to establish a solid support network for their children after moving to a new location. School is a central part of your children's lives, and the more the school staff knows about your children, including the circumstances of the move, the faster they can help them adjust.

This also is a good time to talk to school personnel about the need for and scheduling of tests before, or soon after, your children are enrolled in school. In your role as parent advocate, actively seek assistance from the school and the surrounding community. The more help you receive, the easier it will be for all of you to navigate and feel comfortable with the school and its policies.

If you're a working parent, you'll want to find out about before- and-after-school programs in your area. Even if your children's school does not offer this option, teachers and administrators may still be able to recommend programs elsewhere. And don't overlook the PTA—many schools have newcomers' committees that welcome and provide information to new families.

Class Notes: Some Tips

Here are some tips to help soothe your child's new-school jitters:

- Inquire about pairing your children with buddies who can show them the ropes and sit next to them at lunch.
- Get a map of the school (or make your own) and take your children on a tour before opening day.
- Encourage your children to ask for help (doing so yourself will set a positive example).
- Respect your children's concerns about fashion, speech, and other customs indigenous to their academic environment.

One of a child's most monumental concerns about a new school is whether he or she will make new friends. There are no rules that govern the friend-making process, but having some guidelines can help children navigate this sometimes precarious path. Seeking out new friends doesn't have to be a burdensome task. Kids make new friends all the time regardless of whether they move. Encourage your children to be outgoing and to do the things they always have done to make friends. Here are a few time-tested tips for making friends:

- Arrange play dates with your children's classmates.
- Invite the neighborhood kids over for an "un-birthday" party— no gifts, of course. It's just a chance for everyone to get together and mingle. Hand out inexpensively assembled treat bags, too.
- Find out about after-school activities, like Girl Scouts or soccer practice, that your children might find appealing.
- Sign your children up for classes at area museums or art galleries. Kids love to chatter and become acquainted while they're working on art projects and the like.
- Share some tips that have helped you in the process of making friends: asking questions, extending invitations, being friendly and polite, having a little patience.
- Praise your children for the great efforts they are making toward meeting new people.

It may seem reassuring, but phrases like "things take time" and "things will get better" often don't help adults, much less children. Keep in mind that for a child—especially very young kids—a week seems like a year, and a year seems like a lifetime.

❖

Teenage Territory

While young children might see a move as frightening, teens might see it as downright tragic. Research indicates that adolescent boys have more problems adjusting than any other group. With your help, teenagers may embrace the move as a way to enlarge their lives and create new opportunities. Proper attention and sensitivity to the following concerns can avoid or alleviate potentially significant problems.

Soothing the School Bus Blues

One mother related the following story: After moving to a new community and beginning the school year, her nine-year-old son announced that he wouldn't, under any circumstances, continue to ride the bus to school. For some families, that's worse than a child's boycott on vegetables. Anyway, this caring and resourceful mom dug a little deeper to determine the root cause. Her son proclaimed that the kids on the bus would rather "triple up before they sit next to me!" After piecing together her broken heart, she suggested that they invite one of his fellow passengers over to the house. A date was arranged, the boys became friends, and seating on the bus became a nonissue.

Boost their self-esteem. Assure your teenagers that the difficulties they are experiencing are part of the normal adjustment process and do not reflect any personal failings.

Let them find their way. Be careful not to be too overprotective, and choose instead to give teens the freedom to initiate social activities that help them find their place in the new environment. This doesn't mean you shouldn't give input. Encourage your child to participate in organizations that sound appealing—sports clubs, the yearbook committee, the foreign exchange student group—anything that will give them a chance to meet other kids and become involved in school and after-school activities.

Encourage them to find friends outside of school. For teenagers, making new friends can seem like a monumental task. Remind your teenagers to look for friends outside of school—religious groups are a good place to start. This will broaden their scope of people and reduce some of the pressure to socialize exclusively with fellow students.

If you have arranged for your high school senior to finish the school year in your old location, make sure you keep him or her up-to-date on happenings in and around your new home and community.

❖

In Search of Child Care

Searching for child care can turn a clear-thinking parent into an unhinged wreck. Whether you've relocated to a new area or have lived somewhere all your life, finding quality child care is one of a parent's toughest challenges. With all the extra activities associated with moving, however, the quest for child care that you can live with can be especially daunting. Fortunately, a strong support network exists for parents looking for good child care.

If you have moved because of a job change, enlist the help of your (or your partner's) company. The relocation manager should be able to point you in the right direction. Colleagues are another good source of information.

Start out by asking neighbors. Word-of-mouth referrals are still some of the best consumer safeguards around. Many religious institutions offer child care and after-school programs to con-gregants and other community members. Area colleges and universities, which serve their faculties and staffs, often have additional spaces for families outside the academic communities. They do not always advertise, though, so you need to be vigilant. (I discovered our child care center by accident after reading a small piece in the local town paper about the center's expansion.)

Child Care Aware, a partnership of the Child Care Action Campaign, the National Association of Child Care Resource and Referral Agencies, the National Association for the Education of Young Children, and the National Association for Family Child

Care offers the following five steps for finding quality child care in your area:

1. *Look.* Visit several child care homes or centers before making a decision. Think about your first impression of each place. Ask yourself: Does this place look safe? Is it clean? Are the caregivers/teachers enjoying themselves with the children? Do they talk and play with the kids? Are there enough toys and learning materials to go around?

2. *Listen.* What does the child care setting sound like? Are the kids happy and involved? What about the staff? Do they seem cheerful and patient? Too little noise may mean there is not enough to do. Too much clatter may indicate a lack of control.

3. *Count.* Count the number of children in the group and then count the number of staff. A lower ratio of staff to children means more attention for your child, which is particularly important for babies and younger children.

4. *Ask.* Child care providers should have the necessary knowledge and experience to give your kids the attention they need (and deserve). Do not be shy when it comes to asking about the staff's background. Make sure to include the program director, the caregivers, and anyone else who will have contact with your youngsters. Ask about staff turnover. Inquire about special training required and whether the program is accredited by the National Association for the Education of Young Children or the National Association for Family Child Care. Quality child care providers should be delighted to answer your questions.

5. *Be informed.* Find out what is being done in your new community to improve the quality of child care. Is your caregiver involved with these activities? How can you get involved?

Parents need to rely on their innate perceptions. In the end, you should trust your instincts. Even if you can't put your finger on it, if something bothers you about a particular child care center or home care provider, cross it off your list and keep looking. Something will come up.

Once you do settle on a child care situation, help your little ones ease into the transition by spending time at the center or provider's home, observing and interacting with staff. Get to know the day care provider's environment to educate yourself and to help your children establish trust. This may mean delaying the start of a new job until your children have had a chance to become acclimated to the new day care provider. Easing into the new child care situation is a good way to help infants and very young children adjust to their new surroundings and routine. Think of this period as a long-term investment in your child's future and your peace of mind. Further, children who see their parents interacting comfortably with other adults are more likely to follow suit.

Kid Space That Counts

A child's personal space is sacred. It is not surprising then that a child may be unsettled and even a little frightened by new living quarters. Enthusiasm and some creativity goes a long way toward easing this situation.

Whether it's a move down the hall or to another state, relocating can wreak havoc on a child's emotions. One of the best things you can do after moving to a new house is to provide your child the opportunity to participate in the settling-in process—his or her bedroom is a perfect place to start.

Allow your children to choose where furnishings should be placed—within reason, of course. Providing choices enhances their sense of independence and control. When we give our children the chance to control their surroundings, we're telling them that they can make a difference in the world around them. When my daughter was very small, we had a bedtime deal that worked for a few years. I was the boss when it came to deciding the time. She was the boss of picking out stories. It worked so well that we've incorporated it into other parts of our lives. She felt a sense of control that otherwise would not have occurred if I had not given her a choice.

For very young children, you may want to repeat the arrangement of certain pieces of furniture. For example, if your child's bed was pushed up against the wall in his or her old room, do the same in the new location.

Encouraging children to participate gives them a clear message that their feelings and opinions count. When discussing your children's new rooms, try phrasing questions so that there is no right or wrong answer. You might say something like, "What's a good place for your photos?" or "Where would you like to put your car collection?"

In addition to boosting your children's self-esteem, encouraging their participation and asking for opinions will lead them to take true pride in their environment. Plus, kids who love their rooms are usually more inclined to keep the space tidy. (Of course, *tidy* is a relative term.) But remember, the goal is to have happy kids who are comfortable in their new digs.

Here are some tips for helping your children settle in:

- Arrange young children's rooms first in the new house.
- Always engage your children's help in putting their rooms together.
- Use adhesive wall decorations for a quick and snappy decor.
- Resist the temptation to "throw away the old" (like a blanket or stuffed animal) if your children still have emotional attachments to such items; this will lessen the stress.

Once your children's rooms are set up, celebrate by presenting your junior decorators with a single-use camera, and encourage a photo shoot of the new space. A disposable camera gives kids a tremendous opportunity to express themselves and to share their new environment with old friends. At a time when communication is important, a camera can provide a great outlet for self-expression.

Single-use cameras are easy, inexpensive, and definitely kid-friendly. Pictures can also help tighten the bond between children who have moved and those they left behind. For children who have moved, photographs can be equal to the person being missed.

When Elaine moved from Boston to upstate New York, her daughter, who was six at the time, wanted pictures of her old friends put up immediately. Putting up pictures of their old house made the experience truly a period of transition, allowing her daughter to ease into her new surroundings.

Pictures can give children who have moved a sense of continuity. Moving can be a stressful and decentralizing experience for a young child. Encouraging children to share photographs of the new with friends in the old neighborhood gives them the chance to say, "This is what it looks like. This is how I look," allowing them to connect in very concrete ways.

The period following a move is an excellent time to introduce your children to photography. Pictures give people a visual way to organize their lives. Moving involves so much disorder; looking at pictures of the new place can help children make more sense of the entire experience. In addition, photography can help kids who've moved by showing them how to pay attention to the way they perceive their new world. For a list of books to share with your little shutterbugs, see the Resources section at the end of this book.

Shared Custody and Shifting Homes

For children of divorced parents, a move can be especially devastating. Feelings of abandonment and loss compound the stress normally associated with relocating. The impact on children can be severe whether they are relocating with one of the divorced parents or periodically visiting the parent who has moved away.

Living arrangements that include shared custody, for example, present even more challenges for everyone involved but particularly the child. Even well-meaning parents may overlook a child's personal space. With love, understanding, and some time, parents can lessen some of the emotional turmoil a child may feel.

When children shift from one residence to another, it is important to provide some sense of continuity to allay the effects of being uprooted. When parents can reduce hostility and cooperate with each other, the child's comfort level is more likely to increase. Further, experts suggest that parents provide their children with comforting objects—often those that are most familiar and can travel well.

If appropriate, give your children a sense of connection and rootedness with the noncustodial parent. It's important to convey to children that they have not lost a parent but rather are becoming two-family children; this will help reduce the child's anxiety.

If your children are going to travel from one parent to the other, try to create a comfortable environment in both homes, particularly in the home of the parent who has moved out.

Parents can take specific steps to ensure their children more easily adjust to double living situations. Giving your children opportunities to make choices, for example, can go a long way toward easing the transition. Ask your children what color they want their rooms to be and where they might want to place certain pieces of furniture.

Kid space in the second residence should be appealing and made to feel like a real home, not a place to visit. So try to furnish a room with a bed, or set up a cot with a screen around it if space is limited. Sleep sofas are for guests, not for kids who need to feel comfortable and welcomed.

Taking these extra measures will give your children an added sense of security and permanence. It's a gesture that will also demonstrate your respect for your children's feelings.

For children whose parents remarry, sharing territory with other kids can add another layer of stress. Providing some area of personal refuge becomes even more critical to the transitional child. Try these strategies to infuse a real sense of belonging:

- Create an area that is solely for the child, where his or her belongings cannot be disturbed.
- Encourage the child to carry special toys back and forth and select some that can stay in one place.
- Provide a box that can be locked for mementos and other treasures.

There's No Page Like Home

While books are its main concern, your local library can be a valuable resource for all sorts of community information. Bulletin boards packed with announcements, listings, and schedules greet many patrons before they even walk through the door. You may find free copies of community publications piled high on shelves and tables. Our community library even has a brochure devoted to the moving experience. Be sure to scoop up each and every piece of paper. You can sift through your booty at home and discard whatever you do not need later.

Of course you will also want to check out the stacks. A number of children's books are geared to kids on the move. But do not limit your child's reading material exclusively to moving books. Books about making (and keeping) friends and adapting to new situations can help as well.

Don't be shy about enlisting the help of the children's librarian. This person specializes in helping parents (and kids) find appropriate reading material. If you have time, read, or at least skim, the material first to make sure it is content- and age-appropriate. Books offer many different points of view. A book with a promising title may not always present the desired effect. Once you have decided on some books and have read them with your child, try to talk about the book's content in terms your little one can understand.

Remember, the purpose of introducing these books is to demonstrate coping methods and problem-solving techniques that will help ease your child's transition. And besides, libraries are great fun!

Waaaah!!

A crying baby or toddler—or both—may prevent you from skimming through all the books you'd like to check out. But don't leave empty-handed. Join the leagues of other frazzled parents and grab whatever looks appealing; you can leaf through the books at home without worrying about disturbing the peace. (I always count the number of books so that I'm sure to return the same amount at the end of the borrowing period. Some libraries will even give you a computer print-out of the books you've taken out, to help you keep track of them.)

Staying in Touch

Just as there is no reason to rush children into adjusting to new environments, there is every reason to help your youngster mourn the loss of old friends and other treasures left behind. Communicating with friends from the old neighborhood is a good way to bridge the emotional and physical distance between the old and new. It's especially important for teenagers to not feel disconnected.

Remember that your children's peers are staying behind. That's a big loss for most children at any age. Yet it *is* possible to keep up with the old and seize the new. Here are some easy ways to help your children maintain old ties:

- Purchase or make special address books.
- Provide preaddressed postcards for your children (and their old friends).
- Start a videotape and audiocassette exchange.
- Keep up contact through e-mail.
- Arrange get-togethers with old friends if you're planning a trip to your last location.

Getting Help

Moving-day jitters do not automatically disappear after the first month of settling in. Actually, the "normal" adjustment period varies depending on factors like age, circumstances, and each child's unique disposition. But if you do sense that your children are having difficulties becoming accustomed to the new surroundings, you may want to seek additional support. Watch for the following symptoms:

- Depression
- Lack of appetite
- Increased sleep
- Withdrawal
- Negative feelings communicated through poetry or other outlet
- Acting out
- Inability to focus

In addition to psychologists and other child specialists, school counselors and teachers can be remarkably helpful. Taking the time to meet with them can help you gain perspective and learn how to make the transition easier for your children.

Just like finding a good plumber or a reliable roofer, word-of-mouth referrals are likely to be your best bet when looking for help. Your pediatrician or family doctor should be able to point you to a trained professional who has specific expertise with children in transition. If a new job precipitated your move, try talking with the relocation manager at your new company. In some cases, corporations have contracts with mental health care practices that are accustomed to working with relocated families.

A Little Lonely but Never Alone

No one relishes the upheaval brought on by a move. Everyone's equilibrium is off balance and generally out of whack. Children, in particular, need something to cling to. Often the closest and easiest "object" to grasp is you.

A parent's attitude has a tremendous impact on how well a child will adjust to a move. Yet maintaining a steady, positive outlook is not always possible nor realistic. You are, after all, only human and under stress yourself.

But there is one message that you can deliver to your children over and over again—a message that acts like a trusted tonic. Reassure your children, as they take steps toward making the new more familiar, that they are never alone—that you are with them every step of the way in heart and spirit. This, and your steady love, will help your children become grounded and more secure in their new home and community. It also will underscore the important role you are playing in this young person's life—always an affirming experience for any parent.

❖❖❖❖❖❖❖❖❖❖❖❖❖❖❖❖❖❖❖

Taking Inventory

- Encourage your children to communicate—and then listen to what they say.
- Reassure your children that home is wherever you make it.
- Create a safe haven in your new home by eliminating physical dangers and creating plenty of comfort zones.
- Take field trips in your new town and make every journey an adventure.
- Maintain a steady presence in your children's lives, especially just after moving in.

Chapter 5

Animal House: A Home for the Pets You Love

Animals give us their constant, unjaded faces and
we burden them with our bodies and civilized ordeals.

—Gretel Ehrlich, *The Solace of Open Spaces*

Our cats, Nelson and Amelia, didn't arrive at our new house until the day after we moved in. When they did arrive, we were relieved, but no one was as thrilled as our daughter. While we felt bad for depriving her of her favorite felines, we were glad that they'd been well taken care of and that we hadn't lost them along the way. With a door wide open to accommodate the movers, I had visions of our two indoor, declawed cats venturing out into the unknown wilderness surrounding our new home, totally vulnerable. That was out of the question, so we sent them ahead and had them boarded for a night before joining our family in the new house.

Cats and dogs—even frogs and fish—can sense and react to the stress that is so pervasive during the course of a move. Age plays a role, too, as the older pets are, the more stress they're likely to experience. Adequate and compassionate preparation for your pets can make the transition easier for everyone.

No More Pet Peeves

Minimize moving stress for you and your pet by doing the following:

- Determine your destination state's pet entry laws and regulations by contacting the appropriate state agencies, usually through the department of agriculture.
- Have proper identification tags secured to your pet's collar, including your pet's name and your new address.
- Find out about any pet ordinances that exist in your new location, such as leash laws and poop 'n scoop requirements. Call the city clerk for information.
- Obtain copies of rabies and health certificates and make sure your furry friend is up to date on vaccinations. Some parts of the country are more prone to rabies outbreaks. Make sure you have updated rabies tags, too.
- Become well versed on any diseases for which your pet might be at risk and be on the lookout for hazards like insects, snakes, spiders, and other potentially health-threatening creatures. Be cognizant of terrain changes that may be good breeding grounds for deer ticks, which carry Lyme disease, and mosquitoes, which transmit heartworm and other maladies.
- Don't forget to affix new pet alert stickers near your front door. These stickers clearly direct emergency personnel to save your pets in the event of a fire or other catastrophe.
- Set aside a few items—food or water bowls, special blankets (unwashed), toys, and other familiar objects—that you can have on hand as soon as you move in. If you can, put them in similar spots—litter boxes in the basement, food dishes in a special place in the kitchen. Animals need TLC, too.
- Just as you would help a child adjust, do the same for your pet. For a dog, walk around the yard and neighborhood with a leash. Practice patience, too.

Watch Closely

After moving in, devote some time to close observation. Keep outdoor cats inside until they're well acquainted with their new surroundings. Do this for at least one week. Veterinarians recommend that cat owners keep their felines in one room during that period of introduction. The cat is less likely to escape to the outdoors if it's kept within a confined area. Plus, keeping a cat within one room for the initial period is good preparation for becoming acclimated to the rest of the house.

Restricting your cat to one room may seem unjust. Think of this time as a chance for your cat to get grounded and settled. You might notice abnormal behavior that, with a little time and patience, will pass. We did not follow the one-room rule when we moved and, sure enough, Nelson and Amelia—ever the meowing duo—promptly disappeared into the basement ceiling. Indoor disappearances are preferable to the outdoor equivalent, so be sure to have doors and windows closed before your pets begin their whole-house exploration.

Dogs generally have an easier time adjusting than do cats. However, it's a good rule of thumb to give your dog at least a month during which he can become accustomed to the new homestead. And although it's against the law in many regions to let your dog run free without a leash, you might find yourself in an area where it's okay to let your animals roam. Even so, it's important to give your dog enough time to know where home is. This way, he or she will know where to return for a good meal and a warm bed. Having your dog's old toys nearby will help as well.

Keeping tabs on a dog is a little easier than watching a cat during the phase-in period. While cats are more attached to territory, dogs feel a closer affinity to people and therefore are less likely to disappear into hard-to-find places. In addition to watching your dog's behavior, you'll want to pay close attention to his or her

---

❋

The Vet in Your Life

I've always had a good feeling about the veterinarians in my life. For a variety of cats and dogs, my vets have consistently displayed affection, concern, and a comprehensive understanding of their patients (and their owners). To find a good vet, ask your previous one for a recommendation or contact your local humane society for references. And just as you'd do for yourself, shop around until you find a vet and a practice you're comfortable with. Look for a veterinary practice with waiting and treatment areas that separate cats and dogs, for example. You might even opt for a practice that specializes in cats, dogs, or whatever pets you might own.

---

environment. For example, a dog who's accustomed to carpeting may slide uncontrollably over a linoleum floor. Installing plastic runners could increase a dog's traction and make it easier to get around.

A good diet will also make your pet's life easier. Slowly transitioning your pet's water supply is one way to minimize potential discomfort. Jacque Schultz, behavioral specialist with the American Society for the Prevention of Cruelty to Animals (ASPCA), recommends that you cart along several jugs of water from your old location to your new home. "On the first day, pet owners should provide water from the old location," she says. "On the second day, some of the old water can be mixed with the new water. On the third day, they can offer just the new and watch for any problems."

Cats, who are known for their finicky appetites, may be even more selective during the first few days in their new homes. Though not to be outdone, dogs are creatures of habit as well and, in their own ways, will appreciate the canine cuisine to which they've grown accustomed. You can accommodate their culinary tastes (and avoid a potential feeding disaster) by packing a hefty supply of pet food purchased at your old location. You may find, for example, that Brand X is hard to find in your new area. Rather than trick your pets into something they might find objectionable, simply use some of the old, progressively adding a new brand over time. Veterinarians generally recommend that you take about a week to ten days to achieve the changeover.

Some transitions take more time. Lingering odors left over from previous whiskered dwellers may offend your cats and leave them feeling out of sorts. In our house we experienced the uric acid phenomenon whereby any moisture in the basement activated old, pesky aromas that were offensive to human and feline sensibilities. Eventually, we had the whole carpet removed. That solved the problem. You can also use a deodorizer that's capable of penetrating the bacteria left below the carpet surface.

Kennels, Condos, and Other Temporary Housing

To this day, I still wait until the last minute to make arrangements for someone to look in on our cats when we're out of town. I count myself lucky, though, to have that luxury; a lot of pet owners have no one to turn to, especially if they're new in town. If your lifestyle includes any travel, do some research ahead of time so you're not stuck scrambling for a pet sitter at the 11th hour. Check the yellow pages, ask your new vet for recommendations, and ask your neighbors and new friends for ideas. You may even create a cooperative with others in the same boat.

When Betty relocated from southern California to Oregon, she immediately scouted out places to board her sole family member—her dog Shelley. Her first weekend in Oregon she attended a dog show, where she met breeders and other dog owners who were familiar with the area and what it had to offer. She also checked the classified ads in the Sunday papers. Once she had assembled a list of kennels, she visited each one so she could see for herself which kennel would be best for her dog.

Paws and Imprints

Just as humans feel compelled to make their marks—new wallpaper, a fresh coat of paint—animals, too, like to settle in with an imprint of their own. Cats, especially, want to put their stamp on a new address. Be patient. Litter-box lapses, more-than-usual scratching, marking walls and doors—all are normal behavior as cats make the space their own. "Cats are creatures of routine and prefer a staid environment," says The ASPCA's Jacque Schultz. "People relocating their animals should expect to see that shell-shocked look—ears back, eyes wide, that orphans-from-the-storm look."

Schultz speaks from first-hand experience. When she moved from Queens to Manhattan, she brought with her three cats and four dogs. They were not mutual groomers to begin with and generally steered clear of one another in their daily movements. Once inside her new place, she set them up together in the bathroom. When she checked on them a half hour later, all seven animals were huddled together in the tub.

Just as we take time to adjust to our new environments (and occasionally display slightly unusual behavior) cats and dogs are creatures of habit who need time and space to become acclimated to their change of residence. Give them that period of time so that they, too, can feel welcomed home.

Taking Inventory

- Know your new home state's pet entry laws and regulations.
- Take extra time to help your pet become acclimated to your new home and yard.
- Keep a close eye on your pet's behavior, paying close attention to eating and sleeping habits.
- Find a vet you like and one to whom you can comfortably entrust the health of your pets.
- Affix new pet alert stickers near your front door.

Chapter 6

Recreating Home: Beyond Shelter

A house is no home unless it contain food and
fire for the mind as well as for the body.

—Margaret Fuller, *Woman in the Nineteenth Century*

When we first moved to our current home, I would welcome visitors by giving them a tour, listing one by one all the changes I wanted to make to the house. I wanted to rip out the track lights and install recessed lighting. I wanted to replace the kitchen countertops and so on.

After a while, I set aside my litany of dislikes and, instead, began to watch how my guests responded to the rooms of our lives. Rather than focusing on the poor lighting, they'd see the bright colors of my kids' artwork plastered all over the kitchen. And as I ran in front of their paths to scoop up randomly (and sometimes dangerously) scattered toys, they'd comment on what a great family house we'd bought. As I apologized for the outdated window treatment, they'd remark on the great view through our kitchen window. I finally realized that what was so obvious to our visitors had somehow escaped my perceptions of our two-story colonial: It is the small moments and the priceless possessions of home life that transcend the physical properties of the places where we live.

In these pages you'll learn how to be mindful of the tangible and intangible elements that make a place feel like home. In the chaotic midst of a move—from the moment you know you're leaving to the realization six months later that you have, indeed, a new address—your soul may lose its way from home. It's important, therefore, to have some creature comforts and other treasured belongings to fall back on. Settling in takes time, and in the beginning, your home may feel like a shell. Yet a home can easily be filled to reflect your spirit, ideas, and joys. And it doesn't have to cost a bundle. What's important is to look beyond the practical elements of space and consider the things that truly bring warmth and cheer into your home.

The First Supper

Pizza is usually de rigueur on move-in day, especially if you have helpers to feed. But soon after, try to shake your yen for fast-food. Set up your kitchen and cook something familiar, a real comfort food that's sure to soothe and welcome. Use real plates, too, and make a special toast to your new bounty. In other words, celebrate. You deserve it.

It may be the tulips outside your front door or the glow of a fire that feeds and shelters your inner spirit. For my friend Ann Marie, it is the tree she planted in her yard the year her daughter was born. For you, what matters most might be within the four walls that surround your day-to-day life, from cooking meals to quiet slumber. It is within those walls that we should place that which warms our hearts and sustains our souls. I've always held near and dear a few remembrances from my childhood and other treasures that generally have little monetary value. They are my anchoring devices, belongings that I can put down and pick up again: A clay clown made at camp when I was eight; a pair of blue-and-silver–speckled sunglasses from the third grade. A beat-up, wooden-handled screwdriver that belonged to my father. I may not notice these objects for days at a time. But I know they're here. They're in my heart and soul. And they will stay with me wherever I go.

Tooling around Your New Home

Just before my husband and I were married, my parents presented us with two engagement gifts: a pearl necklace and a fully stocked, fire-engine red toolbox. To my knowledge, my husband has never worn the pearls, but I frequently retrieve items from the toolbox. I can't name most of the tools, yet I am comforted by the notion that they are part of our household arsenal—our metal support system—that helps us hang, remove, tighten, and otherwise perform the basic functions that two somewhat domestically clueless adults can be expected to perform. Naturally, we call in the big guns when a problem arises that would only worsen with our meddling. But for the small stuff, we turn to our beloved red box.

Without this domestic companion, you

- risk spending more money than necessary on repairs,
- miss out on the secure feeling that comes with having a toolbox nearby (even if you use it just once a year), and
- forfeit the opportunity to swap tools with your new neighbors (a great way to get acquainted).

I asked several home improvement experts to come up with a list of tools that would benefit the apartment dweller and homeowner alike. Here's a condensed version of their collective wisdom, including items that won't fit in a toolbox but certainly will improve your quality of life:

- Hammer
- Phillips and flathead screwdrivers
- Wrench
- Pliers
- Duct tape
- Tape measure
- Utility gloves
- Safety glasses or goggles
- Oil
- Power drill
- Putty knife
- Plunger
- Level
- Handsaw

As you shop around for tools, keep in mind that you get what you pay for, so buy tools that are likely to do the job and last for those occasions when you'll need to do the job again.

Protect Your Investment

Just as you safeguard your sense of self in your new home, you must protect the shelter that protects you. Depending upon where you've moved and the age of your home, you will need to prioritize and then perform certain maintenance tasks. Houses, especially older ones, aren't static. "If you've bought an older home, you want to do certain things that will stabilize its systems," says design/build professional Mark Richardson, CR (Certified Remodeler), president of Case Design/Remodeling, Inc., in Bethesda, Maryland. "If there's anything people can do to reduce or stop the deterioration process, they should by all means make that a priority. Let's face it, left on their own, houses don't get any better."

A good place to start stabilizing your home's good health is the home inspection report. Pay attention to anything the inspector flagged. Pay attention as well to obvious signs of deterioration like peeling paint or crumbling bricks on a walkway. Ignoring such signs can lead to costly repairs and the eventual decline of your home. Peeling paint, for example, can result in moisture seeping into the wood, which can cause rot and all sorts of other problems.

If you determine that your home needs major repairs or you're interested in remodeling, take care as you begin to seek professional expertise. In addition to your local yellow pages and better business bureau, there are several ways to find reputable contractors. Word-of-mouth is usually a reliable way to at least add someone to your list of possibilities. Ann Marie Moriarty, former online editor of *Remodeling* magazine, offers the following advice:

- Check out the weekly bulletins for various religious organizations that list sponsors. Sponsors are likely to be strongly involved in the community. Contractors who have won awards for their community involvement usually are good candidates.
- Drive around your neighborhood looking for trucks and dumpsters that are clearly marked with company names. If you're up to it, call your neighbors to inquire about their satisfaction with the work being done. "People love to talk about their remodeling projects," Moriarity says.
- Pay a contractor for two hours of his or her time to assess exactly what your house needs. Be certain to always get reliable references from new friends, local lenders, real estate brokers, building inspectors, lumberyard dealers, and other reputable people in the building industry. Professionals will gladly provide references; it's their best sales tool. You also can contact local chapters of professional societies. Affiliation with groups such as the National Association of the Remodeling Industry or

the National Association of Home Builders Remodelers Council is a good indication of a contractor's professional standing.

• Read the real estate or home design section of your newspaper and look for contractors who have been quoted as experts.

At Home and 20° Below

Relocating to a colder climate can be a chilling experience. Yet before you can warm your heart and soul, you've got to create some real heat. Here are a few easy and money-saving weatherizing tips:

• Cover the window wells to minimize heat loss that occurs through basement windows.
• Apply new putty or caulk around windows.
• Check the condition of weather stripping around exterior doors.
• Change the air filter in your furnace now and monthly during the winter. This will protect the motor and allow the furnace to run more efficiently and cleanly.
• Remove debris from gutters and downspouts. Obstructions can cause water to pool, resulting in ice dams that can ultimately cause interior leaks.

Begin a Domestic Dialogue

Have you ever spoken to a room? Have you ever said good-bye to a house? Have you ever lived in a home that seemed to speak to you? If you've ever experienced these ethereal exchanges, then you know that in order to live harmoniously, you must develop an affinity with your abode. Just as you cultivate relationships with the new people you meet, try to do the same with the home in which you now live.

Strive for Good Feng Shui

Feng Shui (pronounced "fung shway"), the traditional Chinese art of cultivating spiritual power in dwellings by the strategic placement of certain objects, is developing a following everywhere. Feng Shui, which literally means "wind water," reveals how our homes (and work environments, too) can affect our health, relationships, and general well-being. Read up on this ancient wisdom to learn more about how you can incorporate the concept of harmony and space into your new home.

Many of us tremble before the mighty systems that keep a house intact. The big, bad furnace in the basement. The hidden, untrustworthy circuit panel. The toilets that threaten to overflow. As the daughter of a former hardware store owner, I'm embarrassed by these admissions, although I am certain others share my irrational and deep-seated fears.

One of the best ways to overcome fear of the unknown (or of the known but very much disliked) is to approach it head-on. I know—easier said than done. Yet even if you commit to simply giving yourself a tour of your new home and uttering a small "hello" here and there, you'll probably achieve a minimal comfort level. "Hi, furnace," I said when we moved in. "Okay, gotta go." "So *this* is what the underside of a refrigerator looks like," I marveled one morning as I vacuumed all the crud that had accumulated between the kitchen floor and all those coils. "I can do this," I often say, as I'm plunging a toilet that takes on a life of its own.

I admit it. I talk to my house. But like other communication, it helps me understand. It gets me through. Even my son, just three, has begun his own domestic dialogue. Not too long ago, I overheard him conversing with the laundry chute. Every night he throws his dirty clothes down what must seem like a magic tunnel. During this particular one-sided exchange (I couldn't hear what the laundry chute was saying back to him), he would drop something down the two-story vessel and quickly scurry down two long flights of stairs to rediscover what had moments earlier been held by his own small hands. This lasted for at least 30 minutes. It was his way of putting the pieces together and making some sense of the nightly disappearing act.

More people than you probably think have dialogues with their homes. One way to make your place like home is to take that "conversation" one step further by performing a welcoming ceremony. A Native American ritual involves sage, which is lit and then allowed to smolder in the new home. Clare Cooper Marcus, professor of architecture at the University of California, Berkeley, says that sage is used to cleanse a room of its previous inhabitants, removing any memories that don't belong to the new home dwellers. Try this out yourself as you create a clean slate for your new memories. A welcoming ceremony also is a delightful way to make your arrival official.

Open communication between you and your home has practical implications as well. In order to have a meaningful domestic dialogue, building and design experts recommend that you live in your home for a while before tackling any major changes. "A house will talk to you if you let it," asserts Case Design/Remodeling's Mark Richardson. "Houses make noises. The heat kicks on and off. The appliances hum and harmonize. Sound is even reflected from noises caused by neighbors. You may want to add on to a room immediately, yet if you wait you may find that an addition would be better suited elsewhere, perhaps juxtaposed to an area that will yield more privacy."

In addition to its sounds, a home will express the outdoors differently depending upon the time of day and the season. Richardson suggests that people consider living through the change of seasons before diving into a remodeling project. "If you move in the summer or fall, you'll want to wait until the winter to determine how exposed you are." Living in the midst of the upheaval that comes with moving, it's easy to lose sight of what we so easily take for granted, like the privacy and shelter provided by one of nature's best—leaves.

Sunlight is another outdoor element that may not get equal play as you hasten to make your new place feel like home. Atlanta architect Brad Cruikshank agrees with Richardson. "The winter sun is different than the summer sun," he says. "The light it casts changes with the season."

And what about those inhabitants who speak a different language? "Where does the dog like to camp out?" asks Cruikshank. "Can you make a change that will maintain a pet's comfort level and, at the same time, incorporate the needs of people?"

The Light in Your Life

Light—the lack or overabundance of it—can have a profound effect on our moods, outlooks, and ability to become comfortable in our surroundings. If you're light-deprived, for example, you may not function at a level you're accustomed to. Changing a fixture from one that gives off an annoying hum to something less obtrusive can actually eliminate anxious feelings. Some lighting fixtures are intended to stave off the effects of seasonal affective disorder. Other fixtures combine functionality with a pleasing look. Still others are purely decorative. Determining the right light for your life depends on how you want to use the lighting. Cruikshank prefers to light things, not space. "A home's lighting should relate to a function or object," he says. "There should be a point of contact." If you suspect that the lighting in your new home is adversely affecting your attitude, consider bringing in a lighting specialist, someone who has the experience and knowledge to modify your situation in a way that is pleasing and cost-efficient.

Exterior Exception

Make sure any outdoor lighting you buy is specifically approved for outdoor use. Bulbs exposed to inclement weather should be weatherproofed to prevent shattering caused by exposure to rain or snow.

Nothing's Perfect

No matter how hard we try, perfection will always be elusive. Certainly, it's something to strive for. But when it keeps you from moving forward, then it's time to give perfection a rest. When you move into a new home, most things are not perfect. You don't like the color of the walls. The smell is unfamiliar. The purple and silver foil wallpaper gives you a headache. Removing vestiges of the old and incorporating elements of yourself cannot be done overnight. Each change will require your attention, which is often in short supply as you attempt to recreate home.

What should be fun and creative endeavors, unfortunately, become insurmountable projects. "What if I paint the room blue and I don't like it?" you ask yourself. "That chair never looked right in the front hall, but I don't know where else to put it," you say in frustration. "I will never be able to afford to furnish this room the way I want to," you sigh in quiet resignation.

"Where's the coffeemaker?"

Just because you've arrived at your new location doesn't mean that the chaos is over. Packing up is hard enough. Unpacking is jarring as well. It's especially unnerving if you can't find key items—like the coffeemaker or the remote control, or your favorite mug. Rather than succumb to the pervasive sense of urgency, try to relax and build the following into your days:

- Adequate time to initiate and follow a routine
- Periodic breaks from all the turmoil
- Strategies for rekindling elements of what you've left behind (such as the placement of treasured possessions)

Instead of focusing on the labor involved, think about the pleasure you'll derive from a fresh coat of paint in the living room, the serendipitous delight you'll experience by experimenting with the placement of a favorite furnishing. "People shouldn't feel constricted in their new environments," says Joan McCloskey, executive building editor for *Better Homes and Gardens.* "Change stretches us and enables us to breathe new life into everything we do. A chair, for instance, that sat for years in a front hall takes on a whole new context when placed in a bedroom."

Recreating Home, One Room at a Time

After a move it's easy to be overtaken by the chaos and confusion. The thought of setting up every room is simply too much to ask for. You can, however, focus on one room. Set up one room—

with pictures hung, plants placed, photographs of friends and family, and comfortable seating—that serves as a haven from the disruption that unequivocally permeates a relocation.

Out with the Old

It's not unusual for a house or apartment to be neutralized in the selling process. "Neutral decor" screams an ad in the classified section. McCloskey at *Better Homes and Gardens* emphasizes the importance of placing your texture and your smell over the layer that's been left by the previous inhabitants. "Start in the kitchen, where you presumably spend a lot of time," she advises. "Then move on to the bathrooms. Use soaps, shampoos, big, fluffy towels, all the accoutrements that will provide that visceral sense of comfort." Of the five senses, smell is the one most closely associated with memory. If you can recreate a scent that conjures up comfort from your past—freshly baked brownies, burning wood—then by all means infuse your new home and indulge your olfactory sense. It's a subtle but powerful way to help you make your mark.

Your Own Home Spa

What better time to treat yourself to the relaxation and stress-free qualities of a spa? Everyday pressures are particularly felt during the course of a move. Assemble a basket of creams, bath gels, lotions, luxuriant soaps, and sea sponges. Reach for this basket frequently to wash away the anxiety that insidiously wraps itself around the relocation process. Install a dimmer switch to complete the mood.

Flowers can help transform what once belonged to someone else into something that is clearly yours. A window box or a simple vase of daisies can beckon and welcome every time you walk in the door. Flowers are a rite of passage—the senior prom corsage, the arrangement sent in honor of the new baby, a dozen red roses for your favorite valentine. It doesn't take much to cultivate the lighthearted mood that flowers can exude. I try to remember to buy an inexpensive bunch of flowers whenever I shop for food. And if I'm really vigilant, houseguests have a modest arrangement of flowers awaiting their arrival.

The Eddie Bauer catalog makes it easy to keep flowers blooming indoors year-round. Flowering bulbs arrive at your home every month (or less frequently, depending on your order). You may want to try my inexpensive, do-it-yourself method: At the beginning of each month, buy yourself a bouquet of flowers. If necessary, mark it on your calendar. A display of flowers can be as medicinal as the capsules you take to ward off a cold.

Inspiring Comfort

Just as you'd pack a box of sponges and disinfectants for scrubbing your new home into shape, collect your treasures—the things that give you peace of mind—and create a care package for your soul. These are the possessions that will help to lessen the pain of transition and turmoil. It's also the stuff you should unpack *first.* Place your treasures strategically or haphazardly in areas you're most likely to be—the kitchen, the bathroom, the laundry room, even a walk-in closet. Think of these spots as personal shrines for your well-being.

Maybe it's a special picture or vase given as a gift many years ago that will make a room more inviting. You also might consider displaying an object you *didn't* use in your former home. Perhaps an old photograph never emerged from a storage box. Or an old handbag belonging to your grandmother stayed tucked away in a drawer. Moving presents a wonderful opportunity to bring your treasures out for the world to see but particularly for you to enjoy. If you haven't accumulated any special pieces to display, now's a time to start. Just because something is new and store-bought doesn't mean that it can't reflect the deeper feeling of home. Visit a craft store and buy something handmade. Needlepoint pillows, plentiful at home stores, can warm up a room in seconds. Use your imagination and have faith in your instincts.

If you share your home with others, they will want to display, or at least have access to, their talismans. My three-year-old son, for instance, will insist on keeping his bike helmet close by—as an eating and sleeping companion or even to share an episode of "Arthur." Just apply the criteria below:

- Don't feel boxed in by traditional forms of comfort; rules don't apply here.
- Focus on restoring your inner balance, which after a move is generally unsteady.
- Create security in small ways; it is, after all, the small gestures— a light diet of gifts to ourselves—that cheer and console, and ultimately keep us on a relatively steady plane.
- Don't let décor deter you; your shrines, talismans, whatever you call them, need not match a specific design motif.
- Remember, first and foremost, that your talismans are the nourishment you need to reestablish yourself and find peace within your new surroundings.

Set no deadline as you work toward recreating a home that is an expression and extension of yourself. No matter where you live, unless you can be yourself, you will not have a *sense* of self. This is the time to begin to slowly personalize your space, integrating what is psychically important into the physical structure itself.

As I wrote in Chapter 1, uprooting can result in a cascade of losses. When we lose something dear, we feel the void acutely and do what we can to fill it. While you can't always replicate what you've left behind, you can create sacred markers around your space, which will build upon a sanctuary, a place you can call your own. The ability to carry our homes within is what ultimately enables us to make our homes anywhere, anytime. Think of a friend in whose house you always feel at home. Certainly it is something about that person's environment to which you can connect. But it is also your ability to find comfort in that which very simply brings you happiness.

Color with Conviction

It's okay to reject conventional decorating schemes, especially if self-expression is a priority. Offbeat, whimsical, traditional, and contemporary—they're yours to choose from. Decorative accessories that blend comfortably with colorful backdrops can go a long way toward giving you a sense of well-being and belonging. Be courageous with color and give your new home a wake-up call. A flower-clad shower curtain with matching towels can change the hue of a blue winter. Paint an old chest or a chair picked up at a rummage sale for a fun and lighthearted addition. Combine colors, textures, and styles for a truly eclectic pillow arrangement. If you're partial to starry nights, paint a celestial scene in a bedroom. Cover up an old and tired wall with a faux finish. Mix and match, reenergize and renew. You might be pleasantly surprised. And, incidentally, don't get drawn into the "what's hot, what's not" debate; you be the judge.

A Home in Flux

The interaction between your belongings and the home you move into is always in flux. My friend Alice, a painter, rearranges her furniture all the time. "A house is always still," she asserts, "but its objects are movable. When I change the placement of my furniture, I feel renewed. I don't, however, feel compelled to leave it that way. If I want to change it again, then I do. What feels right one month isn't so interesting the next. I know people with collections of art who want everything perfect, so they don't hang anything until they've decided on the perfect spot. Even if they've found that spot, they may want to change it after a month anyway. No spot is perfect forever." The point is to live with what you have. The sooner you surround yourself with the objects you like, the more quickly you become in tune with your environment.

Once you incorporate into your new home the pieces that hold meaning, consider adding new elements that will distinctively identify the space as your own. A blank wall, for instance, may be the perfect canvas for a hand-painted mural. This alternative wall treatment can make a home more memorable and add depth to a room. Check your local newspaper for listings of artists who specialize in murals. Local festivals often feature the work of area artists as well.

A Place for Everything

I confess: I am not the most organized person, which is why I especially appreciate the benefits of having a place for everything. Just as you may have jettisoned unnecessary clutter as you packed up to move, now is the time to get organized. The slate is clean, the time is *now*. I'd rather do anything than organize my belongings, but I will do almost everything to achieve that natural high that comes from living in a manageable environment. Organizing your belongings leads to more productivity and will free you up to get outside and explore your new area. If you're committed to recreating your own manageable space (and want to reduce your clutter quotient), do the following:

- Invest in a few heavy-duty storage containers for the stuff you want to keep (but keep out of sight).
- Organize your files (or hire a specialist to do it for you).
- Plan for storage areas and arrangement of furnishings.

- Before they get lost in the move-in shuffle, place bills, personal correspondence, and other important papers that require your attention in baskets.
- Use a spiral notebook to create a home maintenance notebook (including a schedule for furnace and air-conditioning checks, types of filters used, names and phone numbers of reputable contractors).
- If you've inherited a security system, make sure you know how to use it. (Soon after we moved into our second home, we heard an earsplitting alarm that turned out to come from our house. Up until that point we had no idea the house was wired!)
- Purchase a hook for keys (and hang it up immediately).
- Remember this tried-and-true rule: If you haven't used it or worn it in a year or more, toss it (donate it to a good cause if it's still in reasonable condition).
- Indulge in a couple of junk drawers. (I have two; my daughter has one. Think of these drawers as refuges for the lonely miscellaneous items that can't find a home in some broader category.)
- Consider hiring a professional organizer for a day or a few hours.

Some people live for years in spaces that are cluttered and overrun with unnecessary objects. It may be the slob factor or it just may be one's inability to commit to living in a new space. If you fall into either category, consider becoming more open to change and rethinking what your life is all about. Reorganizing space can actually enrich your life.

✛

Every Home Tells a Story

I recently asked the owner of a popular Virginia inn why the spot is such a popular destination. He explained not with the usual description of services and amenities but in simpler terms that explained the inn's endurance. He told me that every home

Cycles of Change

The Chinese say that you should never keep a picture up for more than a season, because eventually you won't see it anymore. Make a point of changing elements in your new home so that you will continue to see and appreciate all that surrounds you. When life stands still, including the objects with which we come in contact every day, we begin to feel stagnant. Moving things around gives us energy and the ability to see those things in another light.

needs to tell a story. His inn has always been family owned, he said, with some people spending their whole lives there. "Their life stories are here," he said.

Homes really are the embodiment of the people inside—generations gone, generations to come. Human nature pushes us to create living environments in our own image. These environments can become perfect backdrops to your own life story. Start with a cherished object and progress from there. This is a story that can be told over a lifetime.

What Really Matters

I never did replace the track lights in our kitchen, the counters, or the carpeting. Yet next to what's in need of repair are pieces of our lives that resonate with warmth and loving imperfection. Our centerpiece is the fusion of all the things that really matter—the kids' artwork, the unfolded wool and cotton throws, the mile-high stack of school papers, the intangible force that welcomes us back home at the end of each day. As you strive to recreate home, focus on the stuff that really matters, for it is your psychic possessions that will truly be your shelter.

Taking Inventory

- Create a home toolbox with all the essentials.
- Be committed to a good maintenance and repair program.
- Create a balance between practical and more whimsical matters.
- Don't shoot for perfection.
- Don't stick to rules of décor.

Chapter 7

Mastering the Terrain:
Custom Road Maps

> I find the great thing in this world is not so much where
> we stand, as in what direction we are moving.
>
> —Oliver Wendell Holmes, Jr.

*G*etting lost may present unanticipated possibilities: Stumbling upon an auction in progress along a country road; discovering a shortcut to your favorite restaurant; an architectural treasure omitted from a brochure describing an area's interesting sites. These are just a few of the serendipitous outcomes that make getting lost somewhat of an adventure.

On the other hand, getting lost may mean squandered miles on the highway, becoming entangled in a traffic jam, or other undesired scenarios. In this chapter, you'll learn how to master the new terrain and create a custom road map that will get you from here to there and back again.

One of the great things about moving is the open invitation you give to friends and family to "visit anytime." During our first year in the Northeast, we hosted a number of loved ones who usually traveled by air. Picking up and dropping off guests at the small local airport is a cinch. No long lines, ample parking, good location. For me, however, getting back home the way I'd arrived didn't come easy—not until I'd gotten lost for the fifth and final time. After confidently driving to the airport, pulling up to the departure terminal, and saying good-bye, I'd swing around to the exit, make a right then a left. Sad to see them leave, but self-assured that I knew where I was going, I'd tell myself, "This isn't hard. I'm starting to know my way around." And then, like clockwork (remember, I managed to do this *five* times in a row), this self-congratulatory reverie was cut short by the realization that I was headed north, not south toward my home. Inevitably, I'd pull over, struggle with the map, and assure my daughter that Mommy knew exactly where she was and we'd be home in no time. "No time" sort of hung in the air until we actually pulled into the driveway. The last time this misadventure occurred—with my little girl sobbing to get out of the car and me crying in frustration—I vowed that it would not happen again. It didn't. I finally confessed to a neighbor how often I'd made the wrong turn and appealed to her good sense of direction. "Ignore the sign," she instructed me. "You want to turn *right*." That was all I needed to hear.

Learning my way back from the airport certainly enhanced my confidence on the road. It was as if my internal compass had gotten an unexpected and badly needed tune-up. I was ready to roll. But even more astounding was the way in which I began to see the world around me. By finding my way around, I began to establish patterns of what I was supposed to see. I started to say with less frequency, "I'm lost." More important, however, is what I thought: "I'm beginning to like it here."

For many people, unfamiliar territory breeds uncertainty. In a large city, for example, you may lose your sense of place. Until you've carved out a small, manageable area, you may forever feel lost. But I am convinced (and I should know) that it's never too late to become "map literate." Once you know your way around, you can focus on ways in which you and your new community can interact. Establishing a connection between yourself and the area that surrounds you will not only cut down on the number of wrong turns but will also help you bond with your new hometown. By creating your own custom road maps, you will achieve the following:

- Adjust more quickly to all the changes.
- Develop more confidence.
- Rack up a bounty of serendipitous discoveries.
- In spite of feeling fragmented, identify and cultivate a sense of community.

Destination: Anywhere

I don't know a lot of people who like getting lost. Nonetheless, it is a fact of life for anyone venturing into new territory. You know the feeling: According to the odometer, you've gone farther than the two miles you should have gone. You don't see the restaurant where your friend told you to turn left. Nothing looks familiar and you start to feel sick to your stomach. If you're really lost, your hands might be shaking.

When you move, you'll inevitably find yourself hopelessly lost, with little sense of direction, at least a few times. Instead of succumbing to a complete meltdown or even a minor fit of frustration, try to become comfortable with being uncomfortable. It's not the end of the world if you're late, a little flustered, even annoyed. I used to have a boss who would say, "It's only a movie" whenever the pace quickened or a deadline loomed. I don't think life's a movie, really. But I do think that driving around in a new place is sort of like a dress rehearsal for the real thing. So think of your tangential wanderings as a rehearsal for a time when you will know how to get from one place to another. And in the meantime, assume the pioneer spirit and consider your vehicular sojourns as adventures. After all, we're here because of that spirit, and, in a sense, it is what brought you where you are today. Whether they are through wilderness, a desert, or another unfamiliar landscape, your journeys will engender a wisdom that will bring you closer to your terrain, turning what is at first unknown into a place that's solid, tangible, and yours.

One of the most memorable tips I've come across for settling into a new community comes from Jane, who keeps a "destinations notebook" in her car. There she records how she gets from point A to point B and beyond. Jane has moved several times in her life, and wherever she goes she relies heavily on a map and her notebook to get her where she needs to be and back again. She gets up to speed by marking key locations—Kinko's, Office Max, FedEx—directly on her map so that she won't waste time trying to get around. Then she adds stores, restaurants, and any other landmarks that play into her life.

Like most people, Jane prefers to be in control. "I'm not a big adventurer," she confesses, "and the notebook helps me feel secure." There may be other aspects of her life that are out of her control. With the notebook, she has, at the very least, her bearings. Pushing herself even further, Jane applies another strategy for learning her way around. "When I have the time I pick a place I've never been to—the main library, a shopping mall, even the car repair place—and then I force myself to get there and back. Though I don't consider myself an adventurer, I do think of these journeys as adventures."

To create your own destinations notebook, start with an inexpensive spiral-bound notebook found in drugstores and grocery stores. You may want one on the smallish side for easy storage in your glove compartment. Whether it's a rare bookstore you want to find, the great zoo you've heard about, or the way to a new friend's place for lunch, let your notebook be your guide. First, call your destination point to ask for directions. Have a map on hand to help you answer questions like "What cross street are you near?" People who know their way around tend to dispense directions at breakneck speed. Don't be afraid to ask for patience. Tell this road sage that you're new in town and still learning your way around. They'll get the message and probably will slow down. After you've scrawled down your instructions, transcribe them in a readable format onto one page of your destinations notebook. Note your geographic target at the top of the page. If you're really motivated, trace the path on your map with a yellow highlighter. (For the truly goal-oriented, include a table of contents for easy reference.)

For the return trip, just swap a right turn for every left and so on. If you're like me, however, you might experience that left brain/right brain confusion. Instead of confidently arriving back home, you might end up in circles or at a complete standstill. Resist those feelings of inadequacy by simply including in your notebook instructions for a noneventful return trip.

Eventually, you can probably toss the notebook or at least rely on it less frequently. As we learn our way around, the journeys on our custom road map become habitual, a part of our lives that's as second nature as brushing our teeth. It's that comfort level that you want to strive for. And if I can do it, well, let's just say that with a map (and destinations notebook), I'm sure you can do it, too.

Finding Your Niche

A nice way to orient yourself to a new place is to find what you left behind. Let's say you enjoy art and spent much of your time in your previous location visiting galleries and museums. After you've moved, seek out the same. In this way, you blend the familiar with something new and different.

Linda found her bearings by traveling to other people's garages. After moving, she loaded up on maps, town directories, flyers, and her local white and yellow pages. "By far the best thing I did was to drive to garage sales listed in the paper," she says. "This one activity involved reading the paper, using my trusty map, meeting new people, learning my way around, discovering shortcuts, and finding great bargains."

Linda's meanderings led her to friendly, down-to-earth people who enjoyed chatting and offering tips on the best stores, pizza shops, restaurants, and other key spots in her new hometown. Further, these expeditions encouraged her to use a map and drive down streets that she otherwise would not have encountered.

Understanding how things work and knowing where things are will help you combat the uncertainty and even fear that arises when you're surrounded by unfamiliar territory. Take small steps, like Linda, and take pride in your progress. "I've really impressed my husband," she wrote, "with my abilities to get around town, since he basically goes to work, comes home, and runs to the grocery store. And I'm familiar with all the main roads and how they intersect." For Linda, her road warrior instincts took over, enabling her to establish physical and emotional moorings. Free to roam yet tethered to familiar ground, Linda combined courage with a few tools to grow her roots.

Beyond Your Driveway

In writing this book, I asked several people about the meaning of the word *home*. For some, home has little to do with shelter and everything to do with the ways in which they interact with their surrounding communities. Not surprisingly, their experiences conveyed a basic truth—our ability to find our way around is the glue that keeps us connected to our terrains. Alice in Nashville wrote, "Home is that place where day to day tasks mundane efforts like finding milk in the grocery store, knowing where to take your car to be repaired, and having your hair cut—are not a big deal. You know where to go, feel confident about how to get there, and have an expectation based on the past of how these tasks will work out."

For Paul in Brooklyn, home is "when you know the local shortcuts home to beat traffic." A shortcut is like found money—you don't expect it, it makes life a little easier, and (in most cases) you don't have to turn it in for a reward. Adding a shortcut to your destinations notebook is the reward. Even if the shortcut doesn't technically get you there faster, it's still a nice dividend in the business of getting around. In a small but significant way, shortcuts expand your universe, which is a satisfying method for mastering your terrain.

As we explore our terrain, we grow more and more comfortable with each step, each block, each mile. In many instances, however, it's not the ground where we stand but the people with whom we stand who make the terrain our own. Home is running into people you know at the grocery store, the movies, or when you go out to eat. In several communities, the local grocery store is not only the place to pick up bread and eggs, but also the social hub where friends and acquaintances catch up on each other's lives. As you become more entrenched in your community, take advantage of what slowly becomes familiar. When you recognize a face at the drugstore, smile and say hello. If you're outside when the mail is delivered, say thanks to your letter carrier. Initiating with small gestures makes it easier for others to reciprocate and acknowledge your presence. In some situations, you may not want to be noticed and prefer instead to be an observer. As a newcomer, however, anonymity can feel lonely. Once in a while, take a chance. A simple hello or a friendly smile is generally risk-free.

For Sarah, home is less the beautiful Victorian she purchased with her husband in Pittsburgh and more her ability to gauge how long it takes her to get from one place to another. At the start, not only did she get lost, she didn't always know how long it would take to get where she needed to be. Home began to feel more familiar when she stopped driving around in circles, spending entire afternoons doing simple errands.

Even wanting a clean floor might seem like a lot to ask for. What caught one single guy off guard was moving away from everything that was familiar. After moving to the Southeast, Scott wanted to buy a broom. In his previous location, he'd hop in his car, drive to the store, and buy a broom without even thinking about it. What before was second nature suddenly became a conscious act—one that took far more time and energy than Scott had anticipated. But once you've done it—whether you've bought a broom, mailed a care package from the post office, or found your favorite place to buy coffee—it becomes habit. You add wherever it is you've been to your custom road map, and over time the conscious act once again becomes routine, part of the background of life.

A Terrain of Total Strangers

When journalist Mike McIntyre set out to cross the country without even a penny in his pocket, his terrain—his road map—was undefined. He quite literally depended upon the kindness of strangers. Unaccustomed to accepting things from others, he never wanted to be beholden to anyone; he wanted to be the one who gave.

Nonetheless, by putting himself in the way of kindness, he created a traveling community, one that would encircle him over 4,000 miles and through 40 states. And while he put himself at risk by consciously seeking encounters with total strangers, those he met took a chance each time they provided food and shelter. In his own way, he experienced a hypercompressed version of what people who move experience. If he didn't fit into the community—wherever he happened to be on any given day—then he didn't eat, have stories to tell, or have a roof over his head.

In his book, *The Kindness of Strangers: Penniless Across America,* McIntyre chronicles his travels, marveling every now and then at the warmth and trust that surrounded him on his journey. Certainly, there's a lesson for all of us in McIntyre's experience. If we can somehow reach out to others and focus on the possibilities of kindness rather than on the dangers, then our terrains will very possibly be more forgiving, more welcoming, and more quickly lead us home.

Accessible Terrains

If you're physically disabled, mastering the new terrain might be more challenging than for those without disabilities. Unfortunately, even with The Americans with Disabilities Act and this country's increased awareness of disabilities, communities are still beset by barriers that limit people's abilities to effectively interact with their environments.

If your move has presented barriers, such as a lack of ramped entrances or a dearth of interpreters if you're hearing impaired, then your ability to master your terrain will be seriously hindered. Instead of learning to live with it or waiting for the situation to change, determine for yourself what the community is doing to remedy the situation. Newcomers with disabilities should seek help from one of the many freestanding independent living centers scattered throughout the country. Legislated into existence by the Rehabilitation Act of 1973, one-half of each center's board of directors and staff must demonstrate a disability, which speaks well of their commitment to the needs of the disabled. Each center offers an array of services intended to further disabled individuals' self determination. In Rochester, New York, for example, the Center for Independent Living offers architectural barriers consultation by assessing compliance with state and federal access requirements and, in general, helps homeowners and others who want to remove physical barriers to create a more accessible environment.

Taking Inventory

- Buy a couple of good maps; store one at home and one in the car, and refer to them often.
- Create a destinations notebook.
- Seek out your favorite spots—the best coffee shop, the best bookstore, the closest post office—and document your journeys in your notebook.
- Count on getting lost, at least at the start.
- Reach out to others in small ways and put yourself in the path of kindness.

Chapter 8

"Who Will Cut My Hair?" A Community to Call Your Own

It is wonderful how quickly you get used
to things, even the most astonishing.

—Edith Nesbitt, *Five Children and It*

(O)nce you know your way around, it's easier to take steps toward discovering your new community. Finding service providers, places of worship, and stores becomes less burdensome and more enjoyable. You're also more apt to meet people and find your niche. And, more important, you're more likely to start feeling at home. In this chapter, you'll learn how to find what you need to settle in, how to connect with your community and the people in it, and how to make the most of where you are.

A Community by Any Other Name

For some, a community begins on the front porch where passers-by are beckoned to stop for a minute to chat and shoot the breeze. For others, it's the desert where the naked landscape bestows a harmony that the city cannot match. Many so-called "affluent" neighborhoods fail to exude a sense of community, yet some of this country's poorest neighborhoods are inhabited by people who dedicate their lives to promoting strong communities. "Community" does not have a single address. It's everywhere, and, in some cases, it's nowhere. In this age of mobility, many of us must be prepared to pull up our anchors, unfasten our moorings, and leave behind a community we may have truly enjoyed. For some, mobility (or even the possibility of moving) prevents them from embedding themselves into the local community at all.

Remember, though, that a community is not just a place; it's a civic spirit that's comprised of a diverse group of interested parties, including businesses, religious organizations, schools, local government, and private citizens. If rootedness builds stronger communities, does rootlessness necessarily chip away at one's sense of community? I don't think so. Community spirit depends upon people's willingness to get involved. When people speak to each other and join forces to improve their living environment, community spirit thrives. Strong cities and towns are inhabited by people who have a shared sense of responsibility. But just because you leave an area doesn't mean that you leave your values behind. It is possible to reroot yourself into another community and begin a new cycle of involvement. If mobility is a constant threat, it's natural to question the value of making a long-term investment. "Why volunteer and get involved if I'm moving in two years?" you may ask. That's a valid question, but there's another way to look at it. Concentrate on the process—what you learn, who you meet, how you feel. And then remember that if you do happen to move on, you've left an important legacy, whether it's a playground you helped construct, a literacy program you kicked off, or the Girl Scout troop that benefited from your hiking expertise.

Buy Local

In addition to shoring up local economic conditions, small retail establishments can exude community harmony and, in general, a welcoming spirit. In the village of Pittsford, an enclave on the outskirts of Rochester, New York, two stores come to mind. One, the Pittsford Dairy, originally opened its doors in the late 1800s. The other, Montana Mills Bread, is a more recent addition. What the two have in common, however, is their strong presence in the community. The dairy is one of the few places left where you can buy a half gallon or quart of *bottled* milk (returnable, of course). It's also a testament to the loyalty the town has shown toward supporting one of its oldest retail establishments. Montana Mills, which greets everyone with a free slice of bread, is known for its generous contributions to local shelters and food banks. Just standing in line, you can't help but notice the bulletin board layered with thank-you notes from grateful recipients. It feels good to be there, and that's what makes it worthwhile to maybe spend another buck or two on a loaf of bread, or scones or cookies. Supporting local small businesses is an easy way to become connected to your new community. In the long run, you're contributing to economic commerce and are helping to build a strong community. In the short run, you're engaging in the kind of informal public network that ties people to one another and to the community to which they belong.

Many of us equate the best places to live with towns and cities that impart a sense of community. Sometimes I'll see a banner strung across an overpass that's promoting a festival, or a sign that's hung from the side of a building plugging the high school's latest theatrical production. I may not attend the festival or buy tickets for the play, but I feel connected to a larger community, a community that engenders participation and a public sense of integration. Granted, it's not so easy to become embedded into a community, especially if you are a newcomer (and even more so if you know that your residency is a temporary one). But communities are in the business of creating civic engagement, which, in many cases, makes it easy to get involved.

The Butcher, Baker, Candlestick Maker

Do you ever seek out a specific check-out clerk at the grocery store because of her genuine smile? Do you look forward to buying stamps from the postal worker who asks about your daughter who's studying abroad? Is there a hair stylist who really understands your bad hair days? Although they may not be part of our inner circle, these individuals provide a source of social support that helps us get through the days. Certainly, they are service providers who are paid to give us what we need. But they are also what sociologists call "weak ties," who contribute to their customers' sense of community. Mara Adelman, Ph.D., assistant professor of communication at Seattle University, has written extensively on the social support that service providers impart in their day-to-day encounters with consumers. Adelman suggests that when we receive social support from retailers and merchants, at least one of three outcomes occur:

1. Your feelings of uncertainty are reduced.
2. Your self-esteem is improved.
3. You achieve a sense of social connection to others.

It's no wonder, then, that we gravitate toward service providers who put us at ease—whether it's with a smile, a handshake, some unsolicited but useful information, or a simple "thank you." This stuff matters, especially when you're new. So don't underestimate the importance of finding a doctor with a good bedside manner, a hair stylist who won't cut your hair too short, a dentist who understands your low threshold for pain, and a reliable dry cleaner who won't overstarch your shirts.

"Who Does Your Hair?"

For me, aside from getting carded in the grocery store, the highest form of flattery is when someone asks about my hair. I don't know why, but most people—at least the women I know—can recall with complete accuracy every hair tragedy that's ever occurred. This, I am sure, is why we covet good hair salons. Jennifer, a film producer in Los Angeles, counsels her friends who have moved to "find someone whose hair you like, even if it's on the street . . . ask people who does their hair. It works!"

Health Care

Word-of-mouth will probably steer you toward finding good health care and other services that will strengthen your comfort level. If your health care is provided by an HMO, you'll probably need first to scout out a primary-care physician. Ask your neighbors (that's how we found ours), coworkers, and new friends who they go to. Then make an appointment to visit various doctors. Find out what they offer and pay close attention to their communication skills. When you walk out, ask yourself, "Do I want to come back here?" Also, ask doctors where they have hospital privileges and then get the lowdown on those hospitals. Don't be reluctant to visit a facility, especially if you foresee a time in the near future when you will need hospital care (if you're planning to have a baby, to undergo elective surgery, and so on). While you're at it, make sure you know where (and how to get to) the closest hospital in the event of an emergency. Further, post the telephone number of the emergency room in a convenient spot.

Once you've found a doctor and have started visiting the practice, make sure it's still a place where you can be comfortable. Sometimes it takes a few appointments to recognize that your philosophy about health care does not coincide with that of your physician. You may prefer the status quo—continuing the relationship because it's easier than starting all over. On the other hand, it's not a hardship to switch if it means getting better health care. When my friend Robin moved to Kentucky, she needed to find a new obstetrician/gynecologist. She got the name of a physician from a cousin and called to make an appointment. The earliest that she could be seen would be three months away. She reluctantly scheduled the appointment though, like most people, would have preferred to be seen earlier. "I was really annoyed," she recalls, "but I didn't know what else to do. One day in my office a few of us were talking about doctors. I was new at the time, and my colleagues weren't exactly privy to my medical history. Yet as we continued to talk, we shared some fairly private information that seems to have pulled us closer together. I finally shared my frustrations about having to wait so long to be seen by my new doctor. Someone gave me the name and number of another good physician. That doctor agreed to see me within three weeks. Needless to say, I canceled the first appointment."

Here are a few additional guidelines to follow as you seek out quality medical care:

- Have a complete understanding of your health insurance policy; for example, can you select any physician or are you limited by a list of specific providers?
- Ask your previous physician for referrals.
- Consult the local yellow pages.
- Make sure your new physician is board certified. Your physician and the local medical society can verify this information.
- Ask pharmacists about doctors in the area; they may have some insider's knowledge.
- Call your local medical society to obtain names of physicians in your area. A listing there usually means the doctor is a dues-paying member. You'll probably need to gather insurance information and a list of procedures on your own.

- Go online and conduct a thorough search for physicians in your area; you can start by accessing one of the Internet's popular search engines, plugging in key words such as "physicians," plus the name of your new location.

Take a Spiritual Journey

For many movers, getting involved with a church, synagogue, or other place of worship can significantly speed up the adjustment process. Some religious institutions are more welcoming than others. It's important to find the right fit, so don't rush yourself as you seek out a spot for spiritual solace. Take your time. Check things out. You might even church-hop, visiting a different place every week. Whatever you do, talk with other congregants, go to a service, and ask yourself if you can embrace (or at least respectfully tolerate) the institution's philosophies.

When Ken and Suzanne moved to the Southeast, they embarked upon a spiritual journey that included an answering machine. "We wanted to help other Jews coming to the area learn about what was available," explains Ken. "It just seemed natural to install another telephone line and list a number in the phone book." For two years, Ken and Suzanne maintained the "Jewish Community of Coastal Carolina" telephone number, fielding calls from several people, including those who'd come to settle down and even a few who were passing through. It was their way of reaching out and giving back to their new community. As newcomers, they immediately set out to embrace other newcomers—an easy way to begin calling a town your own.

Try Anything Once

Sometimes it takes just one experience to get started. One of the first things I did when we moved to the Northeast was to volunteer for a hospice. I had wanted to do this in our previous location, but couldn't once we decided to move. But I didn't want to give it up. Due to scheduling conflicts, my tenure as a hospice volunteer was short-lived. Nonetheless, the experience was instructive. I learned about a wonderful organization (Advent House), met some truly compassionate individuals, and mastered a few miles of my growing terrain. It also spurred me on to find another volunteer opportunity that meshed well with my responsibilities as a mother.

Here are some ways to master your terrain and, in the process, create custom road maps that will help strengthen your ties to the new place you call home:

Volunteer. The volunteer movement in America is gaining momentum. Opportunities are endless and the rewards are plentiful. There's a galaxy of causes and organizations from which to choose. Giving something of yourself is good for the community and will help you become known. If you like dogs, for example, consider giving time to your local animal shelter. If you have special skills, think about doing pro bono work for a nonprofit group that would benefit from your expertise. If you cared about the environment in your previous location, continue your commitment in your new town. You might also give some time to a philanthropic organization, like the Junior League or your local hospital's fund-raising arm. Volunteering your time to a fund-raising group will help you become an active contributor to your new community and even give your new life there additional meaning. You'll also glean some useful insights from your fellow volunteers who, by the way, will probably be delighted that you've joined their efforts. Remember, though, that while volunteer work is usually free of the trappings and nuisances associated with a paying job, it should always be viewed as a serious endeavor. If you sign up, be there; people will be depending on you. Check your local library, newspaper, or religious institution for volunteer opportunities in your area.

Get involved in local politics. If you like political sparring, tap into the local government. Regardless of your party affiliation, volunteers are usually needed for a number of jobs, from telephone canvassing to staffing voter registration drives.

Take community-sponsored workshops. Adult education classes offer myriad options for fulfilling your thirst to learn and meet others. From art history to Thai cooking, you're likely to find something that piques your interest. You could even teach a course yourself; I've taught a few writing classes that enhanced my knowledge about the community.

Membership has its benefits. If you've got the funds, join a few organizations, such as the local Y or community center. Take out memberships in the local art gallery, museum, or public television station. In most cases, these groups include a monthly (or bimonthly) newsletter that's packed with information about classes, special events, and other ongoing exhibits and programs.

Express your artistic side. A local theater group can help you feel at home, especially if you're a true performer. Read the local entertainment publications, call the drama departments at the local colleges and community centers, look in the yellow pages, or volunteer to usher or sell tickets for a local production. Become a season ticket holder to demonstrate your immediate support.

Get involved with professional groups and associations. Clearly, these are excellent places to network, especially if you're looking for work. Mingling with your professional peers will also clue you in on the local business scuttlebutt. It's one thing to enter into the fray of gossip; it's quite another simply to sit back and listen. You can learn a lot about a place that way. But don't believe everything you hear.

Join a book group. Joining or forming a book group can offer subtle ways for mastering the terrain and creating custom road maps. Going to a meeting gets you out of your own home, forcing you to travel the terrain—often to a different group member's home—for each discussion. The reading and subsequent exchange of ideas can enlarge your mind and become a sort of intellectual road map, one that you can look forward to every six weeks or so (depending upon how often the group meets). Consult your local bookstore to find out if any groups already exist or, like me, start your own. My friend Bea and I launched a group a few years ago. We started out with six and have grown to nearly 15 over time. We all have different outlooks and literary tastes, but we all love to read and discuss books.

Membership May Travel

Before you rip up your old health club membership card, find out if an affiliate exists in your new location. If that's the case, try to strike up a deal that would allow you to renew your membership based on the renewal schedule of your old health club. If you're shopping for a new place to work out, play the smart consumer by checking all your options before signing up. Many health clubs offer one-month memberships at very reasonable rates. Trial memberships allow you to sample the facilities without making a long-term commitment. If you go this route, consider the following points:

- *Hours.* Is the club open when you want to work out?
- *Location.* Is the club convenient to your office or home?
- *Staff.* Are the staff accessible and committed to helping you reach your goals?
- *Clientele.* Are you likely to connect with others or will you feel out of place?

Go to Welcome Wagon® and newcomers club meetings. Welcome Wagon® brought me Holli, a friend who has since moved away, but someone with whom I could relate. We were both new and wanted to meet others. Though I miss her company, we're still in touch, and I'll always have the Welcome Wagon® to thank for making that introduction. I am not by nature a joiner, and you may not be either. But if I'd skipped the orientation meeting (which I did consider), I never would have met my friend. Sure, events that formally pull newcomers together may feel too staged and contrived. But if you concentrate on the potential outcomes, you'll probably have some success. You might even get the name of a good internist or collect some other nugget of information about the community.

Exercise and make friends in the bargain. You can stay in shape and feel connected to your new town by engaging in some athletic activity. Join a gym or a softball league or sign up to play basketball after work. It's not unusual for teammates (or even those from the opposing side) to meet afterward to celebrate a victory (or commiserate over a loss). Check with your department of parks and recreation or the local Y for leagues. Also, ask your neighbors and coworkers if they know of any sporting groups that you could join.

Community Screening

One of the best (and more technically astute) ways to wrap your arms around your new community is to get online. Several Web sites have cropped up over the last few years that are designed to help you become acquainted with Your Town, U.S.A. Microsoft's "Sidewalks," for example, is a growing series of online city guides intended to provide Internet surfers with the flavor of some of our biggest cities. At this writing, ten cities (including Sydney, Australia) are up and running. According to Kevin Eagen, general manager for Seattle Sidewalk, the people behind these sites are, in most cases, themselves long-time residents of the cities included so far. "A Sidewalk site acts as a city concierge," says

Eagen, "that enables people, especially newcomers, to bypass that lengthy period of finding out what's what and where to go."

With some patience, you can find out about movies, restaurants, events, arts and music, sports and recreation, and other places for which a city is particularly known. But prepare yourself for the inevitable advertising that accompanies these free sites.

Your online sojourns should also include sites sponsored by local schools, chambers of commerce, and other organizations located in your surrounding area. No matter where you find yourself, however, you may encounter blips along the way. Don't let high-tech high jinks throw you off the path; even one small find— an usual boutique, a special interest group, a small, undiscovered restaurant—may be all you need to feel just a little more connected to your new community.

Keys and Closings

If your move entailed purchasing new property, you probably worked with a real estate agent. Once you've closed on a house, or, at the very least, received a new set of keys, don't say good-bye to this person too soon. A real estate agent can be a resourceful conduit between you and your new community. Very often an agent is an established resident with numerous ties throughout the area. In fact, it's not unusual for an agent to do things that go beyond the scope of traditional real estate activity. In industry speak, it's called "rounding out." For you, it's a golden opportunity to get the inside scoop on what's happening, who's who, and where to go.

Jamie Columbus, vice president of Judy Columbus, Inc., Real Estate and Relocation, says that a good agent will do more than just provide a housewarming note or gift. "We'll send over the Welcome Wagon® and provide a selective list of doctors, lawyers, and contractors," she says. "Very often we'll start the process before a family actually moves, making introductions to other contacts. We'll follow up on how a relocating spouse is adjusting, we'll ask our friends to acknowledge the newcomers, and, in general, do what's necessary to make them feel welcomed."

It's no secret that real estate agents depend upon repeat or referral business to stay competitive, so it's in their best interest to help you out. But more than that, it is their nature to be outgoing and helpful. Rick Leasure, my former neighbor and president of his own real estate company, expects his clients to stay in touch, and he does the same. "People call all the time," he says, referring to past clients who are seeking information about the community. "I've lived here all my life, so it's not unusual for people to ask for my recommendations regarding various services and companies around town."

Small-Town Bound

Years ago Americans retreated from cities to forge new lives in the suburbs. Today, more and more people are fleeing the 'burbs and exiting the interstates for more bucolic settings in the country. If you're small-town bound, looking for a simpler life, you'll want to take with you certain behaviors and a state of mind intended to help you lead a successful rural existence. Though instead of confining yourself to some murky, unauthored small town code, simply practice good old common sense. Here are a few guidelines.

Don't forget about six degrees of separation. In a small town (or a city that acts like a small town) you never know whose brother, colleague, or cousin you may be talking about. Never underestimate the expansive nature of a well-pruned grapevine. In other words, watch what you say and to whom you say it. In fact, this may be the perfect time to hone your listening skills.

Tone down your expectations for "quaint." In fact, remove the word from your vocabulary. Accompanying the flight to small towns is an extraordinary explosion in technology. The same features that attract people to small towns are enticing cutting-edge companies to relocate to the countryside as well. At first, you may encounter emptier landscapes, lower housing costs, and other treasured discoveries off the beaten track. But sometimes growth brings about a few unexpected side effects—more traffic, less cohesiveness, maybe even more crime than you'd previously thought. The best course of action here is to keep your eyes wide open and consume a weekly dose of reality.

Don't make comparisons. Keep your fascination and love for the city life in check. Saying things like "This place is so small" or "Not a lot to do here, don't you think?" may rile people up a bit and justifiably so. Let the residents—especially natives—know that you're happy to be there and welcome their insights. If they ask about where you're from, then by all means share your story. But don't start out by saying, "Well, where I come from they do things this way." As the saying goes, you'll get nowhere fast.

Arrive with an open mind. It's human nature to judge, even to prejudge. But it's good common sense to keep most of it to yourself, or at least within your family. If you move somewhere anticipating the worst, then that's probably what you'll encounter. If you keep an open mind, however, you'll be less inclined to judge and more influenced by what your new town has to offer.

Seek the advice of others who have come before you. Learn what you can from people who have walked in your shoes, especially with those who do a lot of walking. You might learn something that could in the future prevent you from falling into disfavor or inadvertently alienating another townsperson.

Embedding yourself into a new community is a personal endeavor, especially in a small town. Maybe you'll take my advice and run with a fund-raising group. Or perhaps you will attend a few meetings for newcomers. Your experiences will vary depending upon your state of mind and the people with whom you interact. It's okay to drop out of volunteering or anything you've tried once but find unfulfilling. The key, however, is to not give up. The idea is to keep trying until you find something that truly ties you to the area. You don't have to dig your heels in; just standing around with an open mind is enough. And just because you've chosen the small-town life doesn't mean you must forfeit your privacy or individualism. Understand, however, that anonymity might be a little harder to come by than if you were living in a big city.

Start a Community Bibliography

One of the easiest ways to get the scoop on your new community is to read up on the area. First, get your hands on every free brochure you see. They're available everywhere from the local grocery store to the library. Then subscribe to the local community newspaper. The number of newspapers in your town may vary. If you don't want to subscribe to every publication, ask if you can write a check for a three-month trial period. Some people opt for Sunday subscriptions only, which is better than nothing. If you do this, however, you may miss out on some fun activities, an unusual tidbit about the area, the opening of a new gallery, and other aspects of community life. Remember, you don't have to read everything. My friend Jerry used to tell me the same thing in college whenever she saw me poring over some tome. "Leslie, just read what's really important," she'd say, "the stuff that's likely to be on the exam." It took me a while, but I began to see the wisdom in her advice. I offer you the same, minus the exam—no one's going to test your reading comprehension, but you'll be smarter nonetheless.

In addition to newspapers and brochures, find out if your neighborhood association (if there is one) distributes a newsletter. Even if it comes out just twice a year, a neighborhood newsletter can be a wealth of information. Just reading it can give you a sense of where you'll fit in. Some neighborhood newsletters resemble employee communiqués put out by Fortune 500 companies. Others are more modest and usually feature a single page (front and back) containing essential data like members of the board, messages imploring dog owners to clean up after their pets, block party dates, and anything that may enhance or threaten the neighborhood's peaceful existence.

In many cases, a publication will appeal to its readers by soliciting commentary. We become connected to our communities by reaching out to others. When Linda wrote to me about what she did to feel connected, she closed her letter with the following postscript: "Sending a letter to you is also giving me a sense of community! A letter to the editor or a question to the recipe column can make you feel like part of a bigger picture as well." In this case, writing helped Linda feel in sync with her surroundings. And given the length of her correspondence to me (five pages), her letter probably helped her see for herself how far she'd come. Even a simple written query to your local newspaper can be cathartic.

Paper or Plastic?

If you're accustomed to recycling, you'll probably want to continue this practice in your new location. But don't expect that blue box to miraculously appear at the end of your driveway. Like Lisa of Austin, Texas, your efforts may require a little maneuvering. "I like knowing which way to turn," says Lisa. "It's a good feeling. In the same way I like to know how things work, what the system is. It's disconcerting when what you're used to becomes irrelevant. I thought it was strange at first that we couldn't get a recycling box until we received a utility bill. Then we had to take the utility bill to the local fire station to get a recycling box."

◈

Back to Your Future

Several years ago my mother took me for a ride in downtown Washington, D.C. "I want you to see where I grew up," she said as we headed into her old neighborhoods. I remember with particular clarity one house in which she spent part of her child-hood. On a narrow street with cars parked on either side of us, she stopped and turned to look out her window. For a long time she stared at the two-story row house. It looked identical to all the other row houses. But my mother saw another facade. "But the yard was so big," she said finally, shaking her head in disbelief. Her memory held an expansive landscape, not the postage stamp–sized yard we were both looking at years later.

Our recollections of places may not always be accurate. None-theless, we carry with us an imprint of where we've been. Some-times, we alter or even forget our historical terrains in hopes of accommodating our need to find our way around the territory that's most present in our lives. After Lisa left Rochester, New York, for Austin, Texas, her mental road map of the upstate city became hazy. Talking with another former Rochesterian she met in Austin, Lisa felt as if they were talking about two different places. "It was scary—I couldn't remember names of streets and places," she says. "My mind went blank, and I felt like an impostor, like I'd never really lived in Rochester. At least I haven't forgotten people, but what does it mean when after only three months, I can't remember the names of what were very familiar landmarks?"

Lisa attributed her temporary memory lapse to being in one place at one time. "Maybe it means I've been trying so hard to become comfortable and familiar with Austin that it's taken up all the space in my brain." Indeed, our ability to absorb new terrains can conflict with our need to hold onto our past. During our first year in the Northeast, I missed the Washington, D.C., landscape terribly as well as the very walls that had safely encased me and my family. I used to lie awake at night imagining my geographic past and where I used to live. Many nights I couldn't sleep at all. On one of those nights, during a heavy snowfall, I watched in wonder as a small truck moved up and down several neighbors' driveways. After observing this nocturnal phenomenon for sev-eral minutes, I realized that those neighbors' driveways would be clear when the day began; ours would be heavily blanketed with a night's worth of snow. A snowplow. That's what traveled from the curb up to each house. I'd never seen anything like it; where I came from, people shoveled their own snow.

This snowplow moment—an epiphany, really—was the start of my emergence from denial. I admitted to myself, finally, that I wasn't where I'd come from. I was in a new place, with a different weather pattern, where asking "Who plows your driveway?" is as common as inquiring about the best place to buy paint. Where we come from is where we've been. But where we go and what we do there has as much to do with our past as what the future has in store. Our terrains—our communities—can profoundly affect our lives. If you can hold onto your old terrain and combine your memories of it with promises of something fresh and new, then you will find yourself encircled by a community that is synonymous with home.

Taking Inventory

- Define for yourself what's important about a community.
- Find an outlet that will help you become connected.
- Research your community by reading brochures and pamphlets and by going online.
- Don't underestimate the value of word-of-mouth referrals for everything from physicians to florists to restaurants.
- If you're small-town bound, consider the differences between big-city living and life in the country.

Chapter 9

Friends and Neighbors: A Two-Way Street

Each friend represents a world in us, a world possibly not born until
they arrive, and it is only by this meeting that a new world is born.

—Anaïs Nin, *The Diary of Anaïs Nin,* vol. 2

$\mathcal{M}$any years ago, as my husband and I prepared to move into
our first house, my mother offered this piece of sage and hopeful
wisdom: "In your new neighborhood you will meet other women
who will become your friends. You will watch each others' children grow and be friends for a lifetime."

Well, I did meet other women who eventually became my
friends. I also gave birth to my first child and, indeed, along with
the other mothers, beheld the miraculous annual growth of our
offspring. Yet my mother's words, while comforting at the time,
would years later leave me puzzled and a little blue.

In 1991, as I said good-bye to the women who had generously
shared holiday cookies, parenting advice, and views on encroach-
ing builders and developers, I realized then that my mother's
insight—while well-intentioned—was reminiscent of another
time, a time when more people stayed put, when family members
lived around the corner, and when long distance calls were
reserved for out-of-town cousins.

Parting with my other friends and acquaintances was wrenching, yet I knew we would stay in touch. But how would I replace my neighbors? The people I had come to depend on? The ones whom we trusted to keep a spare key? The people who volunteered in an emergency?

Connecting with others—friends and neighbors—is, indeed, a two-way street. This chapter offers suggestions for walking on both sides of the road. I recognize that this part of settling in can be intensely personal and, clearly, you must do it your way. The tips and strategies on the pages that follow should, therefore, be options that you can take or leave. What's important is that you do what comes naturally and stay true to yourself.

Leaving a Legacy

Laura Herring, president of the Impact Group, a St. Louis–based professional relocation service, urges her clients to put down roots and leave something behind regardless of the duration. "We don't all have to be migrant workers," she opines. Herring believes it's better to connect with people even if that means you may have to say good-bye in the future. "If people allow a time frame to dictate how involved they're going to be in a new community, they're not likely to ever feel connected." Whether it's a friend whose life you've enriched or a committee in town that's benefited from your expertise, leaving a legacy will enrich your own life and the lives you touch.

Our mobile society, coupled with the immense number of working Americans, has changed the landscapes of our neighborhoods. Some people never speak to their neighbors, choosing instead to rely on their workplaces to cultivate and maintain friends and acquaintances. Others draw on their neighborhoods and their work environments to seek companionship. Some simply choose neither, opting to be alone.

But what happens when you don't choose to be alone? What if you move and suddenly find yourself among a sea of strangers whose comings and goings are completely separate from your arrival?

It's easy to dismiss the importance of setting down roots when you're on the move. Why forge relationships when the next move is just two years away? Certainly, for people who don't want to invest in something that seemingly has no long-term benefits, this may be the logical course of action. On the other hand, growing roots has no statute of limitations. That is, you can plant yourself anywhere, anytime.

One summer we hired Rosanna, a gardener, to clear out the debris that had accumulated in our yard over the previous years. I was relieved that, finally, our property would take on a well-cared-for appearance. What stays with me most, however, is the perennial that she transplanted on a whim from the side yard to a garden out front. I was amazed and delighted that something so beautiful could be taken from a safe and nurturing spot to one that offered the same conditions. Her maneuvering might be common in gardening circles, but to me it is metaphorical. Presumably, on its journey the plant took with it nutrients and other sustaining elements, enabling it to continue a long and prosperous life. You can take a similar journey regardless of your destination or the time you plan to stay there.

Today, neighborhoods are as varied as the people who populate them. Some radiate a community spirit of Rockwellian proportions, with block parties, active neighborhood associations, and annual Fourth of July parades. Others are as sterile as a wrapped Band-Aid®, filled with people who barely nod as they get into their cars for their daily commutes. For many newcomers, the days of receiving platefuls of cookies from welcoming neighbors are over.

Others, though, report another story. Rebecca, who moved from Chicago to San Antonio, Texas, almost fell over when she was met on five separate occasions with treats usually reserved for special occasions and special friends. After arriving in Texas, neighbors presented her with brownies, chocolate chip cookies, and strawberry cake. She couldn't believe it.

Risks and Rewards

Sometimes I'll welcome a new neighbor with a loaf of bread. One day last year, before I had made a delivery, I was simultaneously floored and delighted when Susan, a newcomer who has since moved to Atlanta, invited me to her house for lunch. Call it a random act of kindness or one person's way of saying, "I've arrived and I'd like to say 'hello.' " Susan's gesture will forever be appreciated and I will always admire her courage to take a risk on the unknown.

It's not always easy to reach out the way Susan did. Others are overcome with anxiety, relying on an inventory of reasons why they shouldn't intrude, bother, or otherwise pester. Yet you don't need to adhere to a rigid code of etiquette to make your presence known. A good starting place is to be yourself.

It's tempting, though, to erase your emotional slate and start clean. One woman made a conscious effort to change her personality after moving from the Midwest to Boston. "I'd always been 'Kathy,'" she says. "So I thought I'd try 'Katherine.' That didn't last long. In the long run, being true to myself turned out to be just fine."

Once you're comfortable in your own skin it's easier to share yourself with others. Even then you may be haunted by fear. "At first I was very nervous," confesses one globetrotting expatriate whose husband works for a Fortune 500 company. "I needed an outlet, something apart from my children. I wanted to talk to my neighbors, get to know them, but I wasn't sure how to do that. I thought, surely they have their own lives. They were busy and I'd be hard for them."

The Well-Intentioned and Generous of Heart

A colleague once remarked about how bad she felt for overlooking the recent arrival of the family across the street. "The days just go by and I'm so busy. I'd really like to bake some cookies," she lamented. I suggested the loaf of bread approach, which drew wide eyes and a sigh of relief. "That's a great idea," she said. "I would never have considered that." Instead of wondering why you haven't been welcomed, muster up the courage to make the first move. Most people don't mean to be unwelcoming; their lives are simply brimming over with too much to do. It's best to give people the benefit of the doubt.

Though a little apprehensive at the start, this woman began to take the initiative. "I approached my neighbors as people whom I could help. I made cookies, offered to watch someone's kids, that kind of stuff."

While neighbors don't normally provide the esprit de corps that friends so easily supply, they can, nonetheless, help us feel connected—literally—to the ground we walk on. Neighbors gladly open up their bathrooms when your water has been turned off for repairs; neighbors listen to your child's sales pitch for Girl Scout cookies (and even order a box or two); neighbors clear the sidewalk of snow for an entire street just because it feels like the right thing to do.

Here are some easy and nonthreatening ways you can reach out to your new neighbors:

- Look your neighbors in the eye.
- Wave.
- Compliment a neighbor's garden.
- Ask for referrals (best heating contractor, best firewood supplier, best snow plow contractor, etc.).
- Always say "thank you" for any advice you receive.
- Become a volunteer for your neighborhood association (if one exists).
- Offer to take in the mail and newspapers for those going on vacation.
- Accept invitations and reciprocate accordingly.

Party!

When we first moved to the Northeast, I desperately wanted to fit in. Not unlike others who want to understand their new environments, I tried to learn as much as I could about our neighborhood—the people, the history, the character. As the new kid on the block, I had every intention of using that moniker to my advantage. I was too traumatized to invite everyone over for lunch, but I did manage to ingratiate myself into a play group, get on the progressive dinner list, and exchange cookies at the holidays. I was overjoyed by the kindness of my neighbors. Eventually, I stumbled upon an idea to reciprocate: host a Halloween party for the neighborhood kids. Prior to trick-or-treating, the kids stop by—in costume of course—eat a slice or two of pizza, crunch on a few carrots (following my pleas to "eat something healthy"), and then slip into the night to prowl the streets for sweets.

We're not big party-givers or party-goers; my husband and I seem to prefer smaller gatherings. But the Halloween party is one we've hosted just about every year, and every year it is absolute chaos here for about an hour. I was nervous the first few times around: Would anyone come? Would people think I was presump-

tuous to invite mostly strangers for a crazy, somewhat disorga-
nized, event? After a while, though, I realized that the kids (and
therefore their parents) were having a good time. For me, it's the
right thing to do.

> Every neighborhood should have a great lady.
>
> —Jane Austen, *Sanditon*

We have several great ladies in my neighborhood, but
one—Betty—truly stands out. Betty and I met just after my
family moved in. She lives down the street with her husband, Dick, but brought up their two children in another
house around the corner, so she really knows the place.
Her knowledge of the neighborhood, commitment to the
area, and interest in seeing young families move in helped
me find a place here, a place made more warm and welcoming by her guiding hand and generous soul. So, yes,
every neighborhood should have a great lady (or great
gentleman). See if you can find one in yours.

One of my favorite party invitations came from my friend
Sabra. Instead of the usual barn-raising variety, she implored her
friends and neighbors to come to a "porch plummeting" party.
Actually, the invitation was set in a question-and-answer format.
"Longing to destroy something?" You get the idea. Anyway, I
don't think I lifted a finger while we were there; I held fairly
tightly onto my toddler (dodging two-by-fours and other hazards).
But my daughter threw herself into the fray. I was awestruck by
the community of helpers and the spirit of community. Everyone's presence was a tribute to their friendship with Sabra. Certainly, she had reached out to others hoping to get some
assistance tearing down her back porch. Yet less obvious but
clearly apparent was her friends' unconditional generosity.

Love Thy Neighbor's Yard

Talk about pet peeves: When it comes to my yard, nothing annoys me more than people who neglect to clean up after their dogs. It happens very rarely, but when it does, I'm mighty put out. About a year after we moved I spotted through our kitchen this negligent act in progress. "Oh, no," I said, "not this time!" "What are you gonna do, Mom?" asked my daughter, who'd never seen me react so vehemently to a dog doing its business. "I'm going to take this plastic bag and hand it to . . ."

In a pleasant but serious tone I made it clear that leaving my yard without cleaning up was not okay. I also wanted to demonstrate to my daughter that we all must be responsible and take care of our environment. Besides, there's a real risk factor for children who can pick up roundworm if they step in contaminated soil with bare feet. They may experience serious medical problems, even loss of vision. So, all together it's not good for anyone. Incidentally, using a plastic bag is a real cinch. Just put your hand through the bag and use it like a glove to pick up you-know-what. Then invert the bag, tie it up, and throw it away—in your own trash, of course. So, if you have a dog, be sure to respect your neighbor's space.

Giving a party under any circumstances is a test of confidence and endurance. If you shudder at the thought or if you're worried about what people will think of the wallpaper you haven't replaced yet, consider the gesture itself. What better way to say you're happy to make their acquaintance? People don't need extravagance when it comes to new connections. Sometimes just reaching out says volumes about your willingness to be known and to get to know others.

It's Not Who You Know—It's What You Like to Do

Networking is like trying to land your first job. You can't get hired because you don't have any experience. You can't get experience because no one will hire you. Networking presents a similar conundrum: It's difficult to build a network if you don't know anyone. How do you meet people if you don't have a network?

One of the best ways to meet new people is to do what you like to do. If you like to discuss books, join a book group. If you like to cook, enroll in a cooking class. In each case, you probably will meet like-minded individuals with whom you have a built-in, common interest.

Kathleen, a marine biologist by training, loves science and nature. After she moved to the Sonoma Valley in California, she signed up to become a docent for nearby Bouverie Audubon Preserve. There she met several interesting people and received excellent training in natural history.

Kathleen is a master at finding other like-minded individuals. In addition to her fondness for nature, she is interested in books and tends to be drawn to others who like to read. Instead of just browsing in a bookstore, for example, Kathleen will deliberately become friendly with the bookstore owner. Not surprisingly, the bookstore owners put her in touch with others who are as passionate about books (or even specific topics). Kathleen admits that it takes energy and dedication to make connections in this way. Nonetheless, she's become skilled at sorting out who's who in her community.

Stay True to Yourself

If you're willing to sort out the way Kathleen has, you're likely to find a niche, a circle of people—even overlapping circles—with whom you can be yourself. Many years ago, I used to harangue my husband, asking him almost daily, "So, why do you love me, anyway?" After responding with "I just do" or my lazy favorite, "because," he said one day, "Because I can be myself with you."

I've never forgotten his words, and I often use his answer as my own barometer when entering into new relationships. If you can find people with whom you can be yourself, your entire outlook will benefit. You won't worry about offending, slighting, or being embarrassed by the other person, or otherwise alienating yourself and feeling even more out of it than you already do as a newcomer. Remember, too, that some people are simply good at making others feel welcomed. Incidentally, if you try to move the relationship toward something a little more below the surface, you may not achieve the results you're after. Accept this limitation in others; you'll be happier for it in the long run.

If you're unsure about what you like to do, ask yourself the following:

- What have I always liked doing?
- What have I always looked forward to doing?
- What have I done in the past that's led me to meet new people?

Here are some other tips to help you develop a circle of friends and acquaintances:

- Attend lectures and classes.
- Do favors for others. You'll develop a bank full of goodwill, letting people know in subtle ways that you can be counted on.
- Ask for favors; given the opportunity to do a good deed, most people will oblige—it's a good ice-breaker for people who are uncomfortable initiating.
- Volunteer for a worthy cause (but only if you can really commit the time; your good intentions may backfire if you back out).
- Join a book group; bookstores and libraries are a good source for finding the group that's best for you.
- Call your college alumni office for the number of the local alumni club. Then get on the mailing list and go to a meeting or two.
- Get involved in the local political scene. Whether you're a Democrat or a Republican, or somewhere in between, you're likely to find a cause or a candidate that you can get behind.

- Play sports. If you like to play hard, joining a league can be a lot of fun. Check your local department of parks and recreation or your local Y; coworkers and neighbors are also a good source of information.
- If you have children, particularly preschool- and school-age kids, strike up a conversation with other parents; "How do you like the program here?" "Do you know of any good after-school activities?" "How long have you lived in the area?" are just a few conversation openers.
- If you're reluctant to meet people on your own, seek out other newcomers eager to explore the area and meet new people. Traveling in pairs can refract the anxiety that comes with setting out on your own.
- Even if you don't work, carry a "business card" to hand out to people you meet. Include your name, address, and phone number. This will make it easier for people to stay in touch.
- Accept the fact that your offers of friendship may be acknowledged but not readily accepted. Nonetheless, respecting the sensibilities of established residents will, at the very least, demonstrate your patience and self-assuredness.

Small Talk, Big Impressions

Most friendships begin with small talk. Small talk allows us to ease into relationships and get to know one another in nonthreatening ways. So, while small talk may get a bad rap for being shallow, it is, nonetheless, an effective calling card for getting our collective feet in the door of friends, casual acquaintances, and even the people who can make our lives easier (cashiers, bus drivers, etc.)

Naturally, some people are better at it than others. Yet you don't have to be born a smooth talker to reap the benefits of making conversation. Chatting about the mundane is a great way to build rapport—not that questions like "Where do you live?" and "Where did you move from?" will necessarily evoke ordinary responses. But if you become too personal or seem just a little bit intrusive, you risk turning people off completely. Sometimes it's simply awkward for others to talk with people they don't know.

Small talk needs no agenda. Light-hearted conversation should be fun and noncommittal. The trick is to listen well, ask questions, seem interested, and avoid the negative. Use your instincts to determine if a conversation has entered a more serious realm. And respect a person's need for privacy. Finally, know when it's time to retreat.

Sometimes all you need for a little small talk is an introduction by a third party. Often, after people announce their plans to move, someone—a friend, a cousin, a coworker—will inevitably say, "I know someone who lives there. You should call this person. I'll give you the number." Whoa! First, ask your well-intentioned destination services rep something about the person you "should" call. Then, if it sounds promising (or at least a little intriguing), make sure this unsuspecting individual gets a heads-up call before you arrive. Once you settle in and make the call, don't wait for an invitation. Do what Susan did and extend an informal invitation to get together. I've made the mistake of waiting, thinking, "Well, hopefully, she'll call me. We'll become great friends, and she'll introduce me to all the nice people in town." The fantasy used to go on. But now I know that it's okay to reach out. More times than not, it's a risk worth taking for everyone.

A Platoon of Her Own

As a military spouse who has moved 18 times, Kathie subscribed to the maxim, Home is where the heart is—and home is where the Army sends you. She and her family have learned to settle in and become part of the community quickly because they know they won't be there long. Kathie circumvents the short stay by launching a "success team" to wherever she moves. It gives her an instant circle of friends with whom she can share her dreams. "I try to help them as well," she says. "I will never be without one."

To assemble her team, Kathie seeks out people who exude some energy, those likely to put forth some effort to make it successful. It's best to start with seven or eight people, especially since one or two usually drop out. The success team generally meets every two weeks during which time each person can discuss what's going on in his or her life. "We set goals at each meeting and use a kitchen timer so that everyone gets a fair amount of time to talk," says Kathie. "With some meetings we let a natural leader emerge. With others, we rotate among one another. The purpose is to keep us on track." Ultimately, Kathie's success team works because each person is committed to helping the other members move closer to their dreams with ideas, contacts, resources, and brainstorming.

Watering Your Shrinking Violet

Even the most outgoing people are occasionally held back by shyness. Faced with the unfamiliar, our instincts command us to communicate quietly if at all. In a social setting, that could be unfortunate; you may appear aloof and, not surprisingly, keep others at a distance. Here are six steps to help you break through the effects of shyness.

1. RSVP with an affirmative. If you want to overcome shyness, showing up is first and foremost. If you anticipate the worst, you'll fall into the self-fulfilling prophecy trap. Consider upcoming social situations as your classroom, your learning lab. The more you practice, the better it will be. (Incidentally, if you can't go, R.S.V.P. anyway to acknowledge the gesture; no one likes to be ignored.)

2. Imagine the possibilities. Try to keep an open mind about what may lie ahead, what's around the next corner. Shyness can prevent you from taking a leap of faith—a leap that could lead to wonderful discoveries and fulfilling relationships.

3. Be kind to yourself. Shyness and self-doubt are close cousins. It's easy to put yourself down for being shy, but it's healthier and more healing to give yourself credit. Don't dwell on the setbacks. Remind yourself of what went right and make a mental note of how you'll do it differently the next time. Don't waste time beating yourself up over small transgressions.

4. Take one success at a time. Success is addictive. After one we want another and another and another. We move quickly from today's accomplishment to "what's next?" forgetting to savor the moment and congratulate ourselves on a job well done. Racking up achievements becomes the goal, forcing us to forgo what we're trying to do in the first place—in this case, becoming more outgoing. Take the pressure off by planning small, reasonable objectives. Accept an invitation, wave to your next-door neighbor. Next time, accept an invitation and offer to bring a dish; say hello to your neighbor and ask a question or acknowledge the nice day (or rotten, snowy, cold day . . .).

5. Step outside yourself. If you're riddled with self-doubt, your conversation may reflect your discomfort. Focusing on your inadequacies is not the way to get to know others. Rather than point out your faults, concentrate on the people around you. Step outside of yourself and ask questions. Listen attentively. Make eye contact. Compliment now and then. Giving to others is the currency of friendship. Consider the insight of the French actress Sarah Bernhardt: "Life engenders life. Energy creates energy. It is by spending oneself that one becomes rich."

6. Join the club. Very few people succeed in every social situation. A verbal misstep, forgetting someone's name, sharing superfluous information—we all do it and should let "it" go whenever possible. Overcoming shyness—putting yourself out there—takes practice. It's a skill that requires time, examination, and courage.

Friendship Is Hard Work

Most people agree that connecting with others doesn't occur overnight. Indeed, you may "click" with the person across the street or a coworker who shares similar interests. But for the most part, relationships take time to cure. Memories—the fabric of friendships—require a long growing season and can't be hurried. For many, building friendships is a worrisome and vexing process, usually because they're focused on unrealistic and, in many cases, unnecessary outcomes: collecting friends, filling up an address book, waiting for invitations.

For Laura, accumulating friends became stressful. "When I moved, it seemed like a status thing—almost prestigious—to meet and make friends with as many people as possible," she says. "It was too much. Hurt feelings for not being included, worried about excluding others. I was miserable."

Unfortunately, as a newcomer you are not immune to jealousies, rivalries, and other painful elements in the dance of friendship. A new encounter might trigger painful memories from childhood—feelings of rejection, exclusion, even humiliation. The natives may view you as the outsider. Yet all you want is to fit in and be liked—modest goals, really.

But there's that hometown thing: The misconception that you cannot break into established circles because you grew up in another state. Hogwash. Besides, an established circle needn't have originated 20 years ago or more. A circle can start anytime— five years before you arrived or five days after you moved in. The trick is to combine your efforts to reach out with people willing and happy to accept your overtures.

Chart a strategy for finding new friends by adopting the following behaviors:

- Accept differences in others.
- Set aside judgmental thoughts and actions.

- Practice empathy.
- Embrace the unknown.
- Take time to listen and learn.
- Don't come on too strong (or too needy).
- Dismiss stereotypes that can narrow your quest.

Timing Is Everything

The person who doesn't become your friend today may become your friend tomorrow.Considering how busy people are, it's not surprising how little time is left for the pleasures derived from friendships. Before you write off someone as aloof and uninterested, assume his or her plate is full. You never know: You may hook up at a later date.

After her last move, Laura downshifted. "I decided to turn it around. Previously, I'd been advised to meet and greet as many people as possible, to be invited and get invited to as many places as possible," she says. "This time, I was going to proceed at a pace that was right for me. I did this by narrowing in on two people who did become my good friends. I was so much happier."

Other newcomers thrive on a packed social calendar. Holly was determined to learn her new community by extending herself in many directions. As director of media relations for a large corporation, it's her job to know and be known by the local community. "I'm in a visible position, so I need to meet people and know who does what," she says. "For me, it's important to keep my social resumé in circulation.

"And it's not enough to just be invited somewhere," she adds. "You need to go. If you don't go, you may be taken off the list."

Just Say No to Quid Pro Quo

It's tempting to make a mental list of those you have invited over and helped out. It's not surprising that we come to expect people to reciprocate or at the very least to acknowledge our goodwill. This is a dangerous trap that can be avoided by simply doing good for its own sake. Like a good story, just show; don't tell. Folks usually remember your contributions and may even surprise you later on and return the favor.

Give and Take

Most friendships are based on a certain degree of give and take. This is a fairly obvious concept picked up from our early years in school, on the playground, and with brothers and sisters. In a new environment, however, what is normally apparent and clear is suddenly (and uncomfortably) uncertain. Here it is useful to understand what social theorists describe as exchange versus communal relationships.

In social exchange theory, a friendship is a lot like a business relationship. Each party gets something in exchange for something else, not unlike the commerce that occurs between merchants. In this case, however, sentiments and other nontangibles are being exchanged rather than goods and cash.

In a new location it's not unusual to begin relationships on a give-and-take basis. I ask you to join me for coffee; you invite me to lunch the following week. You drive me to the airport; I walk your dog the weekend you're out of town. We each get something out of the deal.

In a communal friendship, there is no "deal." The prize—the gift, really—is the mutual satisfaction that each person derives from the other. In this relationship, we care about each other's welfare.

Unlike an exchange relationship, communal friendships take time, and therein lies the rub: If you've left behind a beloved group of friends (or even just a few), you may be inclined to fill the void as quickly as possible. So instead of investing in long-term relationships, you may focus solely on superficial relationships that can more quickly reduce your loneliness.

"I'll Tell You If You Tell Me"

Remember saying that—in the fourth grade? We may not use those exact words today, yet we generally expect people to reciprocate when we share information about ourselves. "You can't just ask questions," says Evy, a survivor of two corporate moves. "You need to disclose something about yourself. That's how you start to build trust. Otherwise people might perceive that you're too inquisitive and withholding."

In practice that's not such a bad thing. And simply knowing something for what it is can help define where you stand with someone. It's when you fill up your dance card without truly getting to know people that the friend-making process gets stalled. It takes time to become intimate with others. As we reveal more and more about ourselves, we also watch to see if our actions will be reciprocated. That can take a while, so it's best not to rush it.

Regional Variations

Regardless of where you move, you're likely to encounter regional and cultural differences—nuances in the ways people react to your arrival, your attitude, and behaviors. Even neighborhoods within the same urban area will vary depending on the mix of inhabitants. Someone moving from Los Angeles to a small town

Repositioning the Heart on Your Sleeve

You know the saying about wearing your heart on your sleeve. Well, in some cases, it may be better to tuck your heart into a pocket. If you're lonely, for instance, be selective and even miserly with whom you share your emotional state of mind. People tend to withdraw from those who may drag them down. Assuming the speech patterns of the cockeyed optimist isn't necessary either. You've heard it a hundred times before—it's all in your attitude. Make it a positive one and you're likely to attract followers. Focus on the negative and you'll ward off the potential for discovery and ultimate happiness.

Likewise, steer clear of the people who can drag you down: the cynics who complain about the shopping, can't find a decent restaurant, and think the whole town is provincial. Commiserating about the long winters is one thing; uncovering every little imperfection will drive you batty.

in Idaho, for example, may undergo the same amount of culture shock that another individual encounters in another country. Unfortunately, instead of embracing a new culture, some people who are unaccustomed to their new surroundings fall into a trap—inward fear becomes outward arrogance, stymieing any hopes of connecting with the natives (or even others who've relocated).

Many years ago, as an exchange student in Kenya and then Scotland, I learned firsthand how it felt to be a stranger in a strange land. Those experiences and the move to the northeastern U.S. taught me the following basic principles of adjustment:

- Observe first and talk second.
- Be open-minded and flexible.
- Adapt in order to embrace something new.

As you're settling into your new home town and meeting new people, you inevitably will notice similarities and differences between where you've been and where you are now. Condescending comments like, "There's no shopping here" or "How can you stand the weather?" will not endear established residents to you. A meeting of the minds—or finding some common ground—will win you the affection, or at the very least the respect, of the people you meet.

✦

The Ties That Bind

Staying in touch with old friends and acquaintances is a soothing antidote to the loneliness that follows a move. Calling an old friend reinforces bonds, bathes us in fond memories, and comforts our aching hearts. "After we moved away from Philadelphia I used to called my friend, Anne, all the time," says my friend Phyllis. "Talking with her helped me hold on to the familiar. It was very nostalgic."

But as Phyllis discovered, communicating too often with old friends can become a crutch, one that may prevent you from venturing out in your new community. "Sometimes our conversations would leave us both feeling sad," she adds. "Just talking became a stark reminder that we were so separated. The void felt so tangible." Gradually, they spoke less frequently, as each woman tried to fill the empty space left by Phyllis' departure.

Others, however, need the backing and support of old friends to keep loneliness at bay. Barbara has maintained frequent contact with her friend Alice for years. "We've lived here for more than 12 years, and I've never really felt connected," says Barbara. "I called Alice after the first four or five months and told her, 'I'm not making it here.' She really shored me up." Alice, who wanted to "picture" where her friend lived, makes an annual pilgrimage to Barbara's home to reconnect and strengthen a relationship that has survived despite the miles.

Visiting for the holidays is another way to fulfill your need to reconnect. One woman treks back to Maryland from Maine each year for the Jewish high holy days. Others piggyback onto business trips that take them to places in their pasts, reducing the cost of travel. Meeting an old friend at a halfway mark can also ease the financial strain of staying in touch. Reunions, in general, are marvelous excuses to step aside from what one friend calls "an all too much moment," those overwhelming occasions that we'd prefer to avoid.

My husband draws a line between old and new friends. "Old friends provide a deep level of emotional support that cannot be matched," he says. "Old friends give you hope that you will adjust." It is unrealistic, he says, to expect new friends to measure up to what often has taken years to achieve. On the other hand, new friends help us change and grow. Often the people we meet come from diverse backgrounds, which gives us a different perspective than our own.

Old friends tell us, "You can make it." New friends and acquaintances point us in the right direction and can even tell us how to get there. Old friends take you and your emotional baggage in from the cold. New friends see a clean slate and offer you a fresh start.

Too much reliance on old friends may impede your progress. More useful, however, is an old friend's place in your history. Leaving friends helps you understand that life doesn't end after moving away. Try to look at life as a continuum, and carry with you all that you've been, all that you've done, and all that you will do. If friends are important to you, they always will be a common thread on your journey.

Always Keep an Empty Drawer

Entertaining old friends and family in your new home is gratifying and fun. Hosting out-of-town guests can be a decisive moment that clearly confirms your own arrival. "We *must* live here," I used to say to my husband. "We have visitors!" Visitors fill our need to be hospitable. They help define the space around us. And it's in that space—our homes—where we keep the company with those we love. Once you begin to share your home with others, you begin to think of it as your own.

Housecleaning

Moving out and moving in are cleansing. Removing belongings from the old and rearranging them in the new bring order to what generally is a chaotic chore. Similarly, examining your old relationships—sifting out what's worth keeping—can help simplify a cluttered life.

Moving is a particularly good time to consider the friendships that are not working. Losing touch may leave you feeling melancholy or even a little guilty. Allowing the friendship to fade, however, will help you focus on what does work.

P.S. Don't Forget to Write (or Call or E-Mail or Send Gifts)

When I began to e-mail friends and colleagues, my world opened up tenfold. It's true, letter-writing is a fine art and tearing open a letter from a friend is pure joy. Yet logging on to a computer at any time of day without having to look for a stamp is just too easy to pass up. Still, adjusting to new communication patterns is not easy. When we move away from our friends, we acutely miss that they were near—in the office next door, in a house down the street, in an adjoining suburb just ten minutes away. We pine for closeness.

Instead of succumbing to the loss, we can make a conscious effort to begin something new. But changing patterns, especially the way we communicate, requires patience. My friend Chris just got e-mail. I'd been haranguing her to do so for six years. "When are you going to get e-mail?" I'd ask. "You know, you should really have e-mail" and so on. Well, I'm finding it difficult to change the way we've been communicating. I've always picked up the phone to talk with Chris. E-mail doesn't feel sufficient, yet I know it's a good way to express my thoughts without necessarily interrupting her train of thought (which writers are prone to do with their friends). We've agreed to put forth more effort and I have faith that eventually when I hear "You've got mail!" bellowing from my computer, a message from Chris will be forthcoming.

Postscript

Following our move to the Northeast, my family and I did, indeed, find people we could depend on. At least one neighbor at any given time had a spare key. And volunteers always were available in an emergency. Did we replace our friends and neighbors from Washington, D.C.? Not exactly. But year after year we did manage to widen our circle much like a weaver adds threads to create a beautiful tapestry.

Just as places shape our view of the world, people give our lives substance. And while no one has discovered the magic elixir that draws people together, we are all alchemists with the power to discover and then nurture fulfilling relationships. After all, friends really are gold, which is what you get when you transform something common into something precious. But that, too, takes time. So be patient as you extend yourself to your new community of friends and neighbors. People connect in different ways and on different levels. But like the tapestry, a friendship cannot be created overnight; however, when it *is* formed, it is an abundant source of comfort and warmth.

Taking Inventory

- Reach out to your new neighbors in easy and nonthreatening ways.
- Resist the temptation to make unfavorable comparisons between your old and new locations.
- Meet new people by doing what you like to do.
- Recognize that new friendships require time and work.
- Stay true to yourself.

Chapter 10

Moving Solo: Single but Not Alone

I could do very well single for my own part.
A little company, and a pleasant ball now and then,
would be enough for me, if one could be young forever.

—Jane Austen, *The Watsons*

$\mathcal{M}$oving alone is a solo flight. One moment you're soaring, the next you're bracing for turbulence. Perhaps you've moved to be near an aging parent. Or maybe you've followed your heart and, while in the company of love, you're still living the singular life. Possibly you've lost a spouse and want to move on and physically distance yourself from a home that holds too many memories. A divorce might have changed your living arrangements. If you're a new college graduate, you might be setting out on your own for the first time. Regardless of why you've moved, changing locales on your own presents challenges that are not relevant to couples, especially those with children. This chapter will help you understand where your path originates. You also will learn how to map out a clear view of the possibilities ahead.

Make It Safe

Whether you're a male or female, young or old, you'll want to take certain precautions when you move into your new home. The last thing you want to do is appear vulnerable. Here are some tips that will help you stay safe:

- If possible, try to establish a rapport with a new neighbor before move-in day.
- Don't broadcast to the world that you're moving in alone.
- Change your locks immediately and carefully examine other entrances to make sure they're secure.
- Don't put your first name in the phone book; just put L. Smith, for example.
- If you don't have window coverings yet, improvise with sheets or blankets. Don't make it easy for someone to invade your privacy.
- Find out if your neighborhood lends itself to evening activities. Are people out and about after dark or is everyone off the streets and behind closed doors?
- Don't record an outgoing phone message with your name or using "I"; say "We're not available to come to the phone right now . . ."
- If you're meeting someone for a first date, consider doing something during the day in a heavy-traffic area. Dark and remote locations spell uncertainty and could lead to trouble.
- If you're uncomfortable with service people who regularly visit during the initial move-in period (telephone, cable, gas, electricity), arrange to have a friend or trusted neighbor stop by to keep you company. And keep your single status to yourself when chatting with a service person; this applies to in-person and telephone communications as well.

At Work

In addition to college grads, most of whom aren't married, today's work force is comprised of many singles who enjoy their solo status or have lost a spouse due to divorce or death. The 35-year-old single mother or father must contend with visitation rights, school, and other aspects of parenting. Just like families that become entrenched in their communities, so do singles who volunteer, read their local papers, care for their vegetable and flower gardens, and, in general, become deeply connected to their homes and the surrounding areas.

Luckily, companies are recognizing these changing demographics and are beginning to offer services intended to help singles adapt to their new environments. This is great news, though I wouldn't wait for your employer (or prospective employers) to put this progressive thinking into reality. Like anyone who's moved, the onus is on you to do what you have to do to get what you need. And remember, what's not spelled out in a formal written policy can often be agreed upon at management's discretion. Two well-worn mottoes are useful here: "You'll never know unless you ask" and "What's the worst that they can say?"

If you want support, approach your employer and indicate that you're more likely to be happier (and more productive) on the job if you can adjust more quickly to a full and satisfying personal life. Just because you're one and not a family of five should not prevent you from receiving the assistance you need to get socially settled in your new life. Don't accept language implying that because you don't have family ties you don't need the help that an employee with a spouse would request and then receive.

Also, as you develop casual acquaintances at work, don't be afraid to ask your coworkers how you might become more settled in your new town. Naturally, some of your colleagues may not be as congenial as you might like. On the other hand, a few may take you under their wings and even introduce you to their friends outside the office.

When Betty relocated from San Diego, she requested assistance from her employer with little apprehension. When she realized that her dog, Shelley, could not fit in the under-seat dog carrier, Betty opted to rent a car and drive to her new home. Her company paid the bill. The company also hooked her up with Dickinson Consulting Group's Relocation Center, which, among other things, clued Betty in on a dog show that was scheduled three days after her arrival. "I met one of my best friends at that show," says Betty. "Shelley is a shelty and so at the show, I walked around the shelty area and started talking to one of the breeders. I told her where I was living and she said her church was nearby. Then she offered to meet me before Sunday services and take me to the church. I've met other people and it all happened because I went to a dog show."

Turning Everything On

As much as we love our phones and the other utilities that keep us warm, cool, fed, and clean, most of us groan at the thought of getting it all turned on for the first time. If you're single, it's especially burdensome to be home to meet the phone company, the cable representative, or whomever. Being home and waiting around means you're not at work. Some companies give their new employees time off to tend to these pesky move-in chores. Mary, who has always been single, took advantage of all the services her company was willing to offer when she moved. In some cases, she's been very proactive and has asked for the help. Employees are not always aware of their companies' programs and policies. Like Mary, you need to be proactive, even if the matter involves mundane tasks like waiting around for the gas to be turned on.

As companies learn how to more effectively cater to their single transferees, Mary says employees should not be afraid to inquire about how their companies can make things easier. "Employers want you to start right away. It's normal," says Mary, herself a manager of people who have been relocated. "But it takes them six months to hire you, so truly they can probably wait a little longer or at least until you've had time to deal with the practical and physical aspects of moving." Mary suggests that employees build extra time into the transition period during which these chores can be accomplished without interfering with time on the new job. The solution is to put off your start date and be clear with your employer about your needs.

Find a Comrade

A quick way to get settled in the workplace is to find a like-minded single colleague who can relate to your experience. Some companies even have launched formal buddy systems that match new single employees with established workers who are also unmarried or without partners. If you're lucky enough to find a buddy, accept the relationship for what it is. If it blossoms into a friendship, terrific. If it's limited to the exchange of workplace information, so be it. The idea is to learn the ropes in your office, and, if possible, find out people's hot buttons. A buddy can do the following:

- Point out the pitfalls before you fall in.
- Share personal experience so that you don't make the same mistakes.
- Provide a safe sounding board.
- Generally lessen the loneliness that can come from being new.

Creating and Expanding Your Network

You're new in town. You'd like to network, but you don't know where to start. Singles events seem too contrived, and you'd prefer something more informal. Try one or more of the following to help you create a social agenda that keeps your network growing.

Bookstores. Book lovers (and those who pretend) are finding friends and soulmates at special singles gatherings sponsored by some of the larger bookstore chains. If you like to read and want to meet others, a bookstore event can offer both.

Art galleries and museums. Some galleries and museums sponsor singles events, such as lectures, workshops, and special tours. (Even if you don't meet anyone you like, you can always admire the art.)

Fund-raisers. Attending a fund-raising event in your new location is a terrific way to meet people and assess the community's commitment to improving the lives of its inhabitants. The entrance fee is usually tax-deductible. You might even sign up to volunteer for the next event.

Cooking schools and restaurants. Cooking schools offer an informal environment in which to meet others. Restaurants, too, occasionally run special singles-only dinners. If an event is not billed as a singles-only affair, be prepared to meet up with couples. If you don't find programs with singles in mind, inquire if such plans are underway. Your query may be all it takes for a restaurant or cooking school owner to launch a series of singles-only programs.

Parties. Parties for singles let you mingle with and meander around other singles. People are generally there to get hooked up and the numbers can climb rather high. If you can, go with a friend so you can diffuse any feelings of intimidation and split the scene for something better if the evening is a bust. At the very least, it'll be something to laugh about.

Theaters. If you're into drama and enjoy live productions, seek out singles on the stage. Sometimes a theater may sponsor an event that includes watching a production and, afterwards, coffee and dessert.

Don't let one (or even two) bad experiences completely turn you off to singles events. A good evening or a successful afternoon event depends on a lot of things coming together: your good mood, a diverse crowd, an appetizing menu. If you can, be an observer and watch from almost a reporter's point of view. You'll lower your expectations and even discover what you might do differently the next time. Don't view an event as just one more experience. Call it character building, the classroom of life, whatever. The idea is to shop around, shop around some more, and then make some decisions about what you like and how you feel.

Know What You Want

The singles interviewed for this book offered a variety of advice but were unanimous on one point: As you prepare for your move and proceed to settle in, acknowledge what you want. Are you looking strictly for friends? Or are you looking for love? Certainly, the two are not mutually exclusive. Yet unless you recognize the distinction between the two and where you want to put your energies, you may end up running around in circles without anything (or anyone) to show for it.

On the other hand, the singular way of life may just pick up where it left off—only now you'll be somewhere new. Yet even the most gregarious and social people are often rattled when it comes to walking into unfamiliar territory. Unfortunately, loneliness can interfere with your ability to make social inroads. One of the easiest and quickest ways to curtail the loneliness is to let people know you're new in town. For newcomers, battling loneliness can be daunting—especially if you're on your own. That's why it's essential to take advantage of situations that before might have sent you running. "Once you've been somewhere for a while, social events designed just for singles don't seem relevant," says my friend Chris, who's lived on her own for a number of years. "If you're new, though, attending singles functions seems more appropriate, more acceptable."

Contacting a dating service also might seem more acceptable after moving to a new area. For a majority of singles, the bar scene is verboten, taboo, and otherwise not even a blip on their radar screen. If you have no family in the area, introductions through aunts and uncles are not part of the equation. And, according to Nancy Kirsch of It's Just Lunch!, a national dating service, relying on coworkers "wears thin and will run its course." If you do contract with a dating service, make sure its philosophies match your own. Even the people who run this industry admit that dating services have less-than-stellar reputations. Nonetheless, it is possible to meet new people—quite possibly your true love—through a service that's on the up and up. Beware, however, of any company that won't reveal its prices over the phone, says Kirsch. "I wouldn't even think of putting my toe in the door of a place that seemed to be withholding information," she adds. "If you feel like you're getting a line, you probably are."

If you can decide where you fall on the singles continuum, you're one step ahead and more likely to clearly navigate the singles scene in your new locale. Perhaps you're looking for a long-term relationship. Or, you're content to be on your own. Knowing where you fall will help you find what you want in a new location. Networking organizations, singles events, and places of worship are all good places to find like-minded individuals. If you aren't willing to try any of these options because of a negative experience, try to come up with an alternative, something you are willing to do.

Live the Ambivalence

If you're not sure what you want—a long-term commitment or the freedom to be single—learn to act in the presence of ambivalence. Living in the presence of your ambivalence means to pay attention to it. Practice the "act as if" routine; temporarily set aside what you're accustomed to in order to try out something different. It's safe. You're the boss. And there's no commitment.

So you get creative. You brainstorm. You take risks. You do things that normally might seem out of character. Think outside of the box and you might be surprised by the results. Not a joiner? Join something once and maybe you'll change your mind. Never placed a personal ad? Try it once; you might be surprised by the results. Going out on the proverbial limb doesn't mean you can't be selective. Think of it as casting a really wide net, making a voluminous catch, then tossing back what you don't want. It's absolutely okay to say, "Nah, that's not for me." If you limit yourself to meeting and befriending people for the sole purpose of finding a "best" friend (or the perfect intimate companion), you sacrifice the benefits of the learning curve. You shortchange your tastes and your ability to choose. Looking for a soul mate? Then take the time you need to discover and then nurture that relationship.

If you are looking for love, you might as well watch a pot come to a boil. And you know what they say about a watched pot.

First and foremost, get out there and meet people. You might not find Mr. or Ms. Right, but you might become acquainted with someone who could lead you to Mr. or Ms. Maybe. As I wrote in Chapter 9, you're more inclined to meet kindred spirits in places (and in situations) where you truly feel comfortable. Try volunteering once a week for a homeless shelter, and, as an unexpected benefit, meet some wonderful people in the process. You're having fun, you're doing something constructive, and you're widening your circle. Not bad for a few hours' time.

In fact, Kirsch of It's Just Lunch! emphasizes to clients that while a blind date may not advance to lifelong love, it may at the very least lead to a solid friendship. "You might go out with someone who's really attractive and really nice. But do you want to kiss this person? Not necessarily, but a movie would be nice." Just because you've ruled out a romance doesn't mean you can't add this person to your new circle of friends. Remember, each time you connect with a new face and share something of yourself, where you are will, indeed, begin to feel like home. Don't let the *way* you meet someone keep you from letting that person in your life.

Choices You Can Live With

After his divorce, Mike moved from the Northeast to the Midwest to head up distribution for a computer office supply company. While he relies heavily on the phone to stay in touch with his kids, he prefers his weekend visits that provide the in-person contact he craves. To ease the transition, he purchased a townhouse near where his kids live for their Friday-through-Sunday visits. He basically leads two lives, has two sets of friends, two homes.

"But I have only one set of kids, and they are my priority," he says. "It's true that my personal life is less than whole and is at best a short-term venture. I make it very clear to people—friends

Before You RSVP

Just as you might shop around for the best deal in appliances, do some research before showing up at a singles-sponsored event. First, obtain some basic information before simply calling the listed number to say you'll come. Find out something about the sponsoring group, and ask the contact person some very pointed questions, such as the following:

- Who's sponsoring the event and why?
- Who's invited?
- What's the sponsoring organization's track record?

In other words, know what you're getting into!

and prospective partners—that my heart and soul are where my kids are. So I don't have a lot of free time for relationships at this point in my life. When I have time I'm outgoing and gregarious, but for now I've chosen a path that puts restrictions on how much time I can really get connected to my new community. But it's a path I can live with, and that is ultimately what counts."

For Mike, the sacrifices, the trade-offs, are a realistic part of his life's equation. He moved to the Midwest knowing from the outset where he fell in terms of his desire to make a new life for himself. Though he recognizes what he lacks in a social life, he is enriched by the connection he maintains with his children. Talking with him, I got the sense that his journey has not been without a few bumps along the way. "Along with several thousands of dollars in therapy," he says, "I've had to be excruciatingly honest with myself, my family, and people I've met. For me, my success as a parent has depended on it."

One of the most startling aspects of relocation—for singles and couples—is the reality that comes with setting priorities, putting some things on hold, and simply having to wait for things to happen in their own time. Mike has a demanding job and lives by a value system that requires him to limit activities that take him away from his children and his work. But he is hopeful that his life will expand and grow as his children do the same. For now, it's worth the wait.

Pat, a single mother, knew she'd have to put her social life on the back burner after a divorce and move. Even though she was returning to the area where she had grown up and had spent some time as an adult, this time Pat was arriving as a single mother. Drawing on past friendships was not in the cards. "It's easy to say, 'Get out there and meet people,'" says Pat, "but if you don't have good child care or a roster of evening baby-sitters, establishing a social life is nearly impossible. Besides, working and becoming economically independent was my first priority. I simply had to put the other on hold." Pat recognized early on how much energy it would take to reawaken some professional contacts she'd left behind. "It was very challenging to get myself financially grounded and help my daughter adjust at the same time. There was really little time left for anything else."

Pat did manage to get involved at her daughter's school, which offered the added benefit of meeting other parents. Though she missed the social life she previously enjoyed in Ohio, Pat is at peace with the strategy she followed. Shelter, food, clothing—the essentials—were her first priority. Pat says she couldn't have enjoyed a social life anyway with that kind of pressure. Now, she's in a much better frame of mind to really explore the area and the people.

For Kirby, an attorney in Washington, D.C., moving as an adult was a rite of passage. His father had served in the Peace Corps—in West Africa, India, Japan, plus a few cities in the U.S. Though he was accustomed to picking up and moving, the decision to move was his parents', not his own. He attributes some of his success at settling into life in the nation's capital to a life plan he created in 1991. He consciously made a plan for transforming himself from a philosophy student into a downtown D.C. lawyer, and every major move he made afterward was part of his plan. For Kirby, creating and following a plan made it easier to make a place for himself versus taking a reassignment to some random city. Creating the plan empowered Kirby, who finally was on his own, on *his* terms, though I suspect that some of that constant shuffling he experienced at an early age must have helped him adapt to his new environment.

In Search Of

For you, running a personal ad may not sound appealing. On the other hand, if you're open to the hopeful and optimistic adage "You never know," try placing an ad; it may be your route to true love or true friendship. Here are two ads that drew numerous positive responses:

1. From Pam who'd just moved for her first job out of college: "Forming professional singles social group." Though short and to the point, this ad garnered 15 responses from men and women who went on to enjoy a number of activities together. Pam forged a close friendship with at least one of the respondents.
2. From Kathleen who'd just moved to California: "5'8" redhead with brains would like to meet a tall, savvy, successful 40s adventurer. We both love fun, affection, fly-fishing, single malts, animals, Paris, ideas, and travel." Though she did not find the love of her life, this ad opened Kathleen to a number of friendships with men she otherwise might not have met. Some of them even introduced her to other people who helped to widen her circle even more.

As these two women provided the detail of their respective ads, both used phrases like, "I was sort of embarrassed," "It's not something I'd normally do," and "It wasn't so bad." You may not achieve the comfort level you're accustomed to as you venture out, but the results ultimately may put you on a more even keel with being new and single in a strange place.

✦

Suddenly Single

Though divorce is purportedly on the decline, its effects are, nonetheless, quite apparent, especially against the backdrop of a move. Whether you're moving to another state or across town, relocating after divorce with children in tow requires skill, tenacity, and a lot of faith—in something. When Christine, who has split custody (a true 50-50 arrangement) with her ex-husband, moved to another nearby town, she felt tremendously conspicuous whenever she introduced herself to a new neighbor. "I felt embarrassed by my situation," says Christine. "I felt like I had a dirty secret and I had to share it with everyone I met. I just didn't feel okay about it. I'd embarrass myself further by crying to perfect strangers." These perfect strangers, however, are her neighbors and reacted not with shock as she might have expected but with sympathy and understanding.

Christine, who had been married for ten years, had grown accustomed to her role as a wife and partner. Assuming a new identity in a new neighborhood was going to take some time. "I wished everyone just knew so I wouldn't have to pretend. I've learned, though, as I've opened up, that there are other people in my situation. Just knowing that has helped me immensely."

In addition to her decision to be open and honest with the people she met, she decided with her ex-husband to keep their two children in their existing school. "Half the time, the kids are with their father; half the time they are with me," she explains. "Naturally, we wanted to disrupt their lives as little as possible. Keeping them in the schools they are accustomed to seemed like the right thing to do, though it means they don't have that in common with the kids in this neighborhood. But that's okay."

Christine admits that while she loves her new home and looks forward to making it her own, it represents the most significant and tangible aspect of her divorce and finality that her marriage is over. "For me, this move was the result of, and the first major step toward, becoming independent. And the neighborhood has proven to be a good laboratory—a place where I can try meeting people in a natural setting versus one that is more formal like a singles event."

Sharing Space

If you're new in town and looking for a roommate, you'll need to ask some big questions before you agree to share digs. If you're accustomed to living alone, the prospect of sharing space may be unnerving. On the other hand, living with a roommate can open up new social vistas you'd otherwise never encounter. As I mentioned at the start of this chapter, know what you want. Your objective presumably is to find someone with whom you are compatible and who will share the rent (on time). You don't need to be best pals with this person; great friendships have been known to sour once the two parties live under the same roof.

How do you find a roommate? Most large cities have roommate referral agencies that are listed as such in the telephone book. You can also check the papers; bulletin boards at libraries and grocery stores; local real estate offices; Internet sites; college and university housing offices; local places of worship; and of course just about everyone you bump into. You'll become more selective as your search narrows, but in the beginning you'll want to cast your net far and wide.

Once you begin to assemble various candidates, you'll want to refer to a list of lifestyle issues that will help you and your prospective roommate determine if in fact the two (or more) of you can live harmoniously. Even if you discover that you're at opposite extremes, ask yourself if the two styles can coexist. Always keep in mind your likes and dislikes, and be honest about your ability to bend and be flexible. Breaking up is hard to do, especially when you've cosigned a lease.

When you meet for the first time, carefully ask the following questions, allowing enough time for everyone to talk openly and honestly:

- Are you a smoker or nonsmoker?
- Are you a night owl or a morning person?
- What are your quirks (take showers at 3 AM, store strange things in the refrigerator, etc.)?
- Are you extremely neat, somewhat messy, or somewhere in between?
- Do you enjoy visitors, such as frequent overnight guests?
- Do you have pets?
- What are your favorite pastimes?
- How many people do you socialize well with at one time?
- What are your décor preferences?
- Who will pay your rent?
- What kind of food do you like to eat (vegetarian, Kosher, etc.)?

Once you've had an initial interview, use your discussion as a springboard for the next step: establishing ground rules. Be sure to discuss how the two (or more) of you will handle shared supplies like cleaning equipment and food. You might even schedule a weekly heads-up meeting during which you can talk about any concerns that happen to come up over the course of time.

Express Yourself for Yourself

As a solo dweller, there's no need to accommodate anyone else's decorating tastes except your own. Whether you prefer the minimalist look or are drawn to rooms containing many objects and colors, here's your chance to do it your way. Creating a space that's comfortable and welcoming is particularly important for people living on their own.

A few years ago a friend described the dissolution of her marriage. As she reminisced about the crumbling relationship, she spoke, albeit sparingly, with a little hope and even humor. Moving to her own apartment, she had left a household of memories, including the furniture of which she was none too fond. This surprised me, since I'd always admired the pieces that had been hand-built by her then husband. Of course the symbolism did not escape me, though I'd just always assumed it was her style as well. "I always liked that striped wallpaper in your old powder room, Leslie," she confessed. "It was so whimsical. I would have loved to have something like that in my house." As we talked some more, I learned that there was a lot she would have liked to have in that home. I'd always thought of her as someone very ordered, organized, and purposeful in her furnishings and other household effects. "Whimsical" never really came to mind.

I knew she needed to replenish some of the belongings she had left behind and I wanted to be one of the first to help her do so. Something whimsical, I thought. I sent her a set of salt and pepper shakers in the shape of a teapot and teacup. It was a small gesture to signify a big change in my friend's life. Through the mire of divorce and accompanying losses, my friend was making a concerted effort to look ahead. Expressing herself (for herself) is where she began. She has since purchased her own townhouse and, while I've not yet seen her new digs, I am certain that within its walls she has created a space that is truly her own.

Taking Inventory

- Make your new place safe.
- Work with your employer to get the relocation assistance you need.
- Find a comrade at your place of employment who can help you become acclimated to your new work environment.
- Try out a variety of networking opportunities, not just one or two.
- Take time out for simple pleasures and indulgences.

Chapter 11

Retirement and Eldercare: Moving Later in Life

On the front porch of a home . . . these elders constantly
evoke a memory to bridge past times with the present.

—William Ferris, American writer

$\mathcal{I}$ can only imagine my father's expression as he watched my sister and brother-in-law methodically remove old tools, broken radios waiting for repair, and other pieces of his life that had accumulated in our basement. For more than three decades, the basement was a repository for my father's passion—to fix, heal, and otherwise bring back to life that which could not function for one reason or another. Luckily, our neighbors had their own basements to fill up, for it was my father they called upon to fix their broken appliances. My father's proclivity to save projects for a rainy day is in my blood as well, so I can understand how wrenching it must have felt for him to discard his belongings in preparation for a major move.

Whether you're retiring to your dream destination or preparing to move an aging parent, relocating later in life goes beyond the financial and geographic transition. It's true that these two factors alone are often the main criteria people consider as they

191

examine their options. Yet money and locale should not be the only issues to keep in mind. This chapter focuses on the special issues and circumstances that specifically affect people who move in their later years. Here, you'll learn how to incorporate into your life the changes that accompany a retirement move. If you're interested in continued work, you'll also pick up some useful job-seeking skills. For readers preparing to move an aging relative, you'll discover ways to make the transition as seamless as possible.

Preparation Is Key

Unlike a corporate move that can happen quickly with little time for preparation, a retirement move can be well planned and carefully executed. In addition to choosing the right location, you should take a considerable amount of time to determine how this transition will impact your lifestyle—your thoughts about the past, your hopes for the future. Depending upon the reasons for your move, you may overlook this aspect of retirement. Whether you're moving to get out of the cold, be closer to family, or inhabit smaller quarters in the same city, you need to have a clear understanding of your self and the opportunities set before you. Some people begin retirement planning as soon as they start a career. More common, however, is the person in midcareer (or even later) who begins to ponder how his or her "golden years" will be spent. Regardless of when you begin to plan, be sure to give yourself enough time to evaluate your decision. All the research in the world cannot make up for your intuition. If it takes months—or even a couple of years—to decide, that's okay. These days could very well become the best in your life. Don't shortchange yourself by making a rash decision.

Two Places at Once?

Early and late baby boomers will have the ultimate challenge as they prepare for retirement and consider eldercare for their aging parents. Multifamily dwellings may become the preferred housing for people who fall into this category. If this scenario is a likely possibility, certainly factor in everyone's needs but never forfeit your own dreams for a happy retirement. Many of us spend much of our lives trying to please others, often stretching ourselves so that we can be in at least two places at one. Retirement is a time to live life at your own pace without worrying about splitting yourself in two.

Two Couples Think It Over

Helen and Ed knew what they were getting into before they headed to their permanent digs in Virginia. Three years earlier, good friends had preceded them, so they were familiar with the area based on visits and exchanges over the telephone. Ed was in no hurry to pack everything up just because he'd retired. Like Ed, people should not feel obliged or pressured to pick up and leave simply because they've stopped working.

Helen and Ed knew what they were looking for: a college town, access to the arts, a more temperate climate, a strong Jewish community, and smaller quarters. Ed had always wanted to go to college, so the academic offerings in the new town made it even more appealing. An octogenarian, he was the oldest one in the classrooms, though, not surprisingly, he managed to obtain two degrees, one in applied science in marketing and a B.A. in art history.

Having friends in the area certainly gave Helen and Ed a head start in adjusting to their new community. Friends helped make inroads into the area, though Helen became involved in her own right, helping to get the area's Hadassah group off the ground and doing other activities that eventually would widen her circle.

A year ago Linda and Sam traded in New York state's snowy winters for Florida's steady warmth. They, too, knew something about the area and how it would suit their physical and emotional requirements. They had vacationed often in Sarasota and were familiar with what it had to offer. But they also knew that they didn't want to be snowbirds. If you're six months in one place and six months in another, you may not feel connected to either place. As a result, they began to cut back on their obligations and withdraw from some of their activities up north. They eventually decided to put down an anchor in one place. They wanted to take root, establish some grounding, and give something to the community. They chose Florida.

As Linda and Sam scouted out a place to live, they decided early on to move into quarters that would be comparable to the space they enjoyed up north. Heeding their friends' advice to avoid moving into a place that was too small, they held on to their belongings and sought housing that would accommodate their kids and grandchildren. Eventually, Linda and Sam decided to build a home with enough space for them and rooms to spare for visitors.

Where to build became the next question. During their visits they noticed that people who originally had retired to Barrier Island were moving again—this time to the mainland. Dealing with bridges and traffic is generally a part of the vacation equation. Living in a recreational area full time is another story. Linda and Sam weren't up for that. What you might deem charming on a vacation could very well become an inconvenient nuisance year-round. It's important, therefore, to change lenses and look at an area not as a visitor with a camera in tow but as a resident who must deal with parking permits, taxes, and insurance expenses.

Reality Check

If you're thinking about retiring to be closer to children or grandchildren, or have already done so, remember that they have created lives that are separate from your own. Most likely, they'll be tickled to have you nearby. Nonetheless, you should not expect them to incorporate your life into theirs. "I was never in my kids' backyards before retiring," says one woman whose children and grandchildren do not live close by. "I don't feel a need to change in that regard." Also, keep in mind that while you may have more free time, your children's calendars will fill up fairly quickly. Prior to moving closer to family, carefully evaluate your relationships. Ask yourself:

- How much time am I willing to give my family?
- What is my relationship with my family and how will it change when we live closer together?
- What do I need in the way of social interaction with my peers?
- Do I want to work part-time (or full-time)?

❖

Housing for the Good (and Easy) Life

Where you decide to retire will depend on the circumstances leading up to your retirement. If you've lost a spouse, for example, and find yourself suddenly single, you may need to distance yourself not only from the home you shared with your partner but the entire geographic area as well. Maybe the mere thought of shoveling snow brings on a migraine. Perhaps you're going to live on wheels and travel the country. Or like Linda and Sam, you're reviewing blueprints for a brand new home. You've probably heard of the three most important issues in real estate: "location, location, location." In addition to scouting out a site for your living quarters, you should include, to a large extent, the type of housing that will best suit your present and future needs.

"Too often, retirement-aged people select housing that strictly accommodates their current needs," says Erica Karp, MSW, founder of Northshore Eldercare Management in Evanston, Illinois. "A townhouse with stairs may be very appealing in the short term, but later on navigating two levels could be unwieldy and too demanding." Think ahead to a time when you might need more flexibility in your daily life. Before you fall in love with a design that won't accommodate your changing needs, consider an environment that will make life easier, not more difficult. For example, look at housing that incorporates universal design, encompassing features intended to be used by everyone regardless of their abilities. Such features might include door handles that do not require gripping or twisting to operate, living space limited to one floor, audible and visual alarm systems, adjustable-height kitchen counters, and wider passageways.

Looking ahead to the future is healthy and exciting. Making plans for what is presumably the last third of your life, however, has a sobering effect that would dampen anyone's outlook—at least temporarily. Mortality, which many of us squirrel away into our subconscious, suddenly plays a bigger role as you contemplate retirement. That doesn't mean you should add your name to the nursing home waiting list. It does mean that you should consider your options carefully before following someone else's lead or doing what your children think is best. Opting for the middle ground will prevent you from making costly errors in terms of your finances and emotions. Since it's unlikely that you'll want to move again, take your time, especially if two of you are involved in the decision. If one of you wants to stay and the other wants to move, try to confront your differences by finding some common ground. Common ground usually requires compromise on both sides. And while you may not reach a true win-win situation—each may end up losing something along the way—you will have come to the decision together. Be prepared to discuss how you're going to pare down on space. Some people must sell a portion of their library collections. Others regretfully part with oversized antiques. Questions like, "Who gets to keep what?" and "What must we give up?" are tough but must be addressed.

In some circumstances, the questions are never asked. Arline describes a move that in many respects was heartbreaking but essential. She lived in the same home for 83 years. The kitchen had served as a makeshift operating room when her tonsils were removed. A memorial service for her mother took place in the living room—funeral homes didn't exist yet. Arline was even married there. But after her husband developed terminal cancer, they decided to move out. Her husband wanted her to be settled in another place before he died. "He didn't want me to be burdened with this big house," she says. Married for 58 years, this couple truly planned ahead. In the strictest sense, their move was a major transition. But for Arline it was more of a gesture, a gift from her husband. "We were very close and it was certainly hard to leave," she recalls, "but his illness and the anticipation of losing him weighed much more heavily than the actual move."

Prior to the onset of her husband's cancer, Arline found her physical world changing as well. In 1991, an ice storm severely damaged two of the couple's largest trees—one in the front yard, another in the back. "It really ruined our yard," she says, "and somehow that made it easier to leave." For Arline and her husband, it was time to surrender to one of life's inevitable outcomes. Despite her husband's illness and the accompanying anxiety and worry, this couple still knew what they needed. They secured housing, easing her husband's peace of mind and significantly reducing the burdens typical of home ownership. In 1993, they moved to an apartment situated within a senior living and nursing home community. The move did nothing to curtail their independence and did everything to help them get through a painful and precarious time and enjoy their last months together.

For a time after losing her husband, Arline was cloaked in grief, mourning not just one loss but many. Clearly, she believes in something bigger, something beyond her control. "I don't know why, and I don't know how," she muses, "but it struck me that things were in place, that I had done the right thing." Today, Arline stays busy, volunteering a few mornings doing office work, and keeping company with some of her neighbors. "We don't sit on people's doorsteps," she says, "but we have found in each other soulmates—companions who bring simple joys."

Never Stop Planning

If you're preparing to retire and relocate, or have already reached your retirement destination, conduct an audit of your life. A comprehensive life plan is a practical tool that will help you keep on track. Geriatric care managers and others in the retirement field can help you devise a plan that includes financial, insurance, housing, health care, and legal issues. Most self-assessment exercises are a little painful—it's not the questions we fear; it's our answers. Nonetheless, it's easier to prepare a plan when you're in reasonably good health. If you wait until your health deteriorates, you narrow your options and make what could have been an organized effort into one that is haphazard and poorly executed. And remember, a plan is rarely set in stone. Indeed, some of the best laid plans change for the better.

My friend Betty, who is 76 and will move with her husband into a retirement community in the coming months, is looking forward to a similar circumstance. "I've been in this neighborhood for 40 years, and I'll miss most things about it—the trees, the people, the character," she admits. "But being in a neighborhood with people so much younger can be somewhat isolating. I'm looking forward to being in the company of people with whom I can more easily relate.

"On the other hand, I'm likely to experience some real culture shock. When I've been there to visit, all I see are old people," she says with a laugh.

Your choice of housing is as varied as your interests, dreams, and needs. Only you can decide what's best for your particular circumstances. Knowing what's available, however, will jump-start the decision-making process. Housing needs for older Americans are always under review. Government organizations and private groups are working together to improve housing options for seniors. Here's a quick glimpse of what you can expect to find as you begin to research the retirement housing market. Keep in mind that the information presented in these pages is strictly a snapshot view; your research should extend to other books and materials that are devoted exclusively to the topic.

As you inquire about real estate, retirement communities, and other housing options, you'll be inundated with literature featuring glossy photographs and enticing descriptions intended to sell you on the spot. Before you sign anything, even before you consult an attorney, test-drive what feels appealing. Visit the area several times. Talk to others who have made the move before you. You may balk at the very sound of "retirement community." A closer inspection of the amenities, however, may reveal an appealing environment. If you've always dreamed of hitting the road, then by all means get the lowdown on motor homes; just be sure to *do your research.*

Seeking Shelter

Now more than ever seniors have a virtual housing galaxy from which to choose. Builders are becoming wise insofar as designing houses that can grow and adapt with their inhabitants. The health care industry has taken notice by creating and managing assisted living complexes that can accommodate a wide range of needs. The most important rule of the housing game is to research your options. You might even decide that you should stay

---

Definitely Doggish, Feline Friendly

If you plan to move with your pet, make sure you know the policy on keeping animals. Many apartments and condominium complexes strictly forbid residents from having cats and dogs. If you have to part with your beloved furry friend, arrange for an adoption that will ensure your pet's health and safety and your peace of mind.

---

put, at least for the time being. That's okay. You'll probably save yourself a lot of money and heartache, too. Here are some reasons you might want to move:

- Your loved ones have moved on.
- Your current home is more than you can handle and too costly to maintain.
- Your current home doesn't match your lifestyle anymore. You're tired of stairs and would like all your living space to be on one floor.
- You want to tap into the capital that's tied up in your home.
- You've outgrown your neighborhood.
- The climate is starting to get to you.
- Your community doesn't adequately cater to your needs.
- Your community can no longer accommodate your health and medical care requirements.

What's Out There?

Before you venture out on your own in search of appropriate housing, consider the value of working with an experienced real estate agent. It's best to find an agent who specializes in your needs. Referrals can come from friends, family, mortgage lenders, title company representatives, or real estate attorneys. Here are a few popular retirement housing alternatives.

Single-family homes. You may purchase the home of your dreams, but remember to buy the house that's right for you. Determine what you really need. If you're willing to reduce your living space, make sure you keep all your furnishings in mind—moving furniture from a 2,300-square-foot colonial into a 900-square-foot cottage might leave little room for anything else! Before you buy, find out if houses in the neighborhood are appreciating in value. Also, with the help of a reputable home inspector, determine how well the home is built. Often what you can't see turns out to be the most expensive to repair. Don't forget about the trash: Who collects it and how much does it cost?

Home-sharing. My mother grew up in a house that sheltered three generations. Today, of course, families are scattered everywhere, and some folks find one family challenging enough. Two retiring couples, however, may benefit from living in a collaborative home that combines private space with common areas. You can share expenses and look forward to built-in companionship. On the other hand, you could drive each other crazy and ruin an otherwise wonderful relationship. So tread carefully as you consider this housing option.

Condominiums. A few years ago, when my mother told me excitedly that she and my father were finally going to sell their house and buy a condominium, I was less than thrilled. Theirs was the only home I could remember from my childhood. Every room, especially my old bedroom, held memories that could never be replaced, especially by a high-rise building containing single-floor dwellings. But for my parents, a condo held the promise of home ownership without the burdensome maintenance. It was the right choice for them. Of course condos can be low-rise garden apartments or townhouses. Generally, you don't need to mow the lawn and recreational facilities are often plentiful. If you're accustomed to walking out the front door for a neighborly stroll around the block, be prepared for a different sort of outing at a condo; the location you select may not be offer this kind of environment.

Mobile homes. For people on a limited budget, mobile homes are an economical housing alternative. You can "anchor" a mobile home in a special park, on your own land, or on your children's property. In recent years, mobile home parks—especially for retirees—have sprung up all over the country. Like the options mentioned above, you'll want to fully understand the amenities and limitations of mobile home living before you make your selection.

A Space of Your Own

If you're relocating with a mate, try to create separate spaces. Years of cohabitating in larger quarters is habit-forming. And it's not unusual to take our private space for granted. That's why it's a good idea to designate two areas—one for you and one for your spouse or partner—where solitude, quiet, and privacy are generally guaranteed and always respected. It does wonders for a relationship and will help ease the transition.

Retirement communities. Retirement communities offer a range of housing environments from independent living to settings that provide a full range of health care services. These communities also feature comprehensive security services, meals, and a host of activities. Because they are so inclusive in terms of the amenities, it's possible that you might feel claustrophobic—emotionally and physically. Before choosing a retirement community, ask yourself if you'd feel confined after a living there a while. Make sure, too, that the residents are people with whom you can relate.

✥

Your Favorite Work

Some retirees don't retire at all. They just do something different, whether it's to start a new business, pursue a college or graduate school degree, or volunteer for a worthy cause. Whatever you do, it should be your favorite work. Maybe you've spent a lifetime doing something you're glad to be finished with. Or perhaps you enjoyed your work so much that you'd like to do the same for the community on a pro bono (and less frequent) basis. Supplemental income isn't a bad thing either. In the meantime, if dropping out of the workforce is not your idea of retirement, rest assured that there are many options from which to choose. The tight labor market has made employment among older people a little more plentiful. Older workers who once might not have been considered are now falling into favor among some employers. Remember, however, that by working, you will lose some of your Social Security benefits, unless you're over 70. Be sure to check with your accountant before starting a new job—full- or part-time.

If you're interested in working in your new location, review Chapter 2 for some helpful tips. Most job-hunting tips are universal and, in today's tight labor market, may apply to all age groups.

One of the best options is to find temporary work. Temporary jobs provide flexibility, prevent you from becoming tethered to one employer, and can supplement your income nicely. Today, more and more employment agencies are recognizing the value of adding seniors to their rosters. Mature Temporaries is a nonprofit employment agency that focuses on placing workers in their 50s, 60s, 70s, and up. The Akron, Ohio–based organization finds jobs for former machinists, teachers, accountants—you name it. If you can't find such a firm in your area, approach some others, pitching yourself as someone who can add a seasoned perspective to their list of workers. Paul Magnus, director of Mature Temporaries, counsels senior job seekers to hook up with a job club, which generally pulls together a group of people looking for work. A facilitator keeps the group focused and helps to create an environment in which people can learn from each other. Check your local department of labor for information about job clubs.

You'll also want to prepare for what all job-seekers contend with: rejection. Employers tend to divide people into two groups: people who will be bothered by your age and those who won't. Those who don't factor in your age are more likely to hire you based on your ability to do the job. Naturally, you'll want to avoid the former and obtain as many introductions to the latter as possible. As you ponder the professional landscape, consider the possibilities in the following list. They may not send you, but perhaps something on the list will inspire you to look further and ultimately find the work that's best suited to your new lifestyle. Good luck!

- Bed-and-breakfast operator
- Tour guide
- Massage therapist
- Writer
- House-sitter
- Pet-sitter
- Nanny
- In-home health care provider
- Mystery shopper (employed by companies to shop around and snoop on the selling strategies of their competition)
- Library assistant
- Administrator for a nonprofit organization

Taking Care of Others

For many of us, eldercare is intangible, something other people deal with. Most of my contemporaries are still knee-deep in Barbie dolls, soccer practice, and after-school playdates. Even when my father became ill it was my mother who stopped working to provide the care he needed. It's simply impossible to forecast when we'll need eldercare services. Yet as the baby boomers age, more and more of us are going to face the eldercare dilemma.

Moving Back

A solid career in California didn't keep Alice from returning to her Tennessee roots to care for her mother. After her father died, Alice and her husband, Jim, left San Jose for Nashville. "Once my father died, the guilt of being so far away from my mother increased exponentially," says Alice. "I didn't want to be dependent on airplanes to get home. I needed to be able to jump in a car. My husband just happened to get a job in Nashville." At the time, her mother lived in Memphis, a few hours away by car but considerably closer than the cross-country distance Alice had traveled previously.

Today, her mother, 67, lives directly across the street in the same Nashville development where her daughter and son in-law reside. Now if her mother needs help, Alice can do so in the same time zone *and* get back to her job without having to make up for days off the job. "It was definitely an adjustment to be living so close to my mother, especially for my husband. Who would've thought he'd be living across the street from his mother in-law? But I'm comforted by the fact that we can help her and help her stay out of trouble. She was always the handy one, climbing on the roof to remove a branch or lifting heavy yard equipment. It's hard for someone to give that up, but I think we've made it easier by being so accessible. Plus, she has a lot of independence. I don't clean her house or fix her meals, but I do take her to the grocery store and my husband is always amenable to lifting, climbing and doing chores that are simply too much for her to be bothered with. We do have rules, though. My mother, for instance, was the one who insisted that no one comes visiting without calling first.

"I think we give her peace of mind as well. She once asked me if I'd answer the phone in the middle of the night. I said, 'Of course,' and that seemed to put her at ease. That's really what I've wanted, so I'm actually very grateful it's turned out this way."

Never the Road Alone

Eldercare experts (and caregivers themselves) counsel caregivers to make time for themselves and to solicit help from friends, family members, and neighbors. Caring for an aging relative can be confining and stressful and lead to burnout, which is really about feeling out of control. If you suspect that you are suffering from burnout or sense that your situation is taking on a life of its own, stand back and reassess the scenario. Consult the Resources section at the end of this book and keep telling yourself, "I'm not alone."

Following Your Heart

For Patrice, moving from the West Coast to the Southeast held the possibility of strengthening and to some extent changing her relationship with her parents. When her parents first retired, they settled in a community where one of Patrice's brothers lived. Her parents and six siblings felt secure by the fact that a family member was nearby. Unfortunately, her brother's business took a downturn and, subsequently, he left the area. What started as a solid and sensible solution quickly became a tenuous and troubling situation. "I was the logical choice to take over my brother's role," explains Patrice. "There are six kids in the family and most are married with kids. I'm single, which means the uprooting would involve only one person. Plus, I had some personal reasons for going. A few years ago, I watched many of my friends lose one or both of their parents. Strong, successful people were falling apart—freaking out—and voicing regret in some cases. I didn't want to be in that position, at least I don't want to have many regrets where my parents are concerned. I wanted to have time with my parents during which we could really get to know each other and like each other as adults. I wanted to create an atmosphere where that relationship could be based on friendship and respect. I never truly had that before, so I saw this as an opportunity to sort of rectify it."

Moving an Aging Relative

Under most circumstances it's probably best for an older person to stay put and connected with what's familiar. An established support system, especially for an elderly person, isn't easy to replace. If you must move an older relative, you'll want to research eldercare resources in the community you're moving to. But first you must do some serious soul searching. Denise Brown, publisher of *Caregiver* newsletter, cites a ten-step decision-making process first developed by medical ethics researchers. Going through the process will help prospective caregivers feel better about decisions they make. The following steps also will help you face the gut-wrenching and guilt-laden emotions commonly associated with caregiving decisions:

1. *Review the situation.* Get the facts on both sides—where your aging relative falls on the health care continuum and where you are in your life (personal aspirations, professional life, relationships).
2. *Gather additional information.* Consult health care professionals and ask for ideas from friends and family. Can they provide another perspective? Can they share their own experiences?
3. *Identify the ethical issues.* Should you let your fiercely independent mother continue to drive even though you know she could endanger herself and others? What arc your moral obligations to your relative? To society at large?

4. *Identify the personal and professional values.* Do this both for yourself and your relative. Including this person in the decision-making process is crucial. Think about how you would feel if someone were making a decision on your behalf, without your consent or knowledge—probably not very good. Respect is key.

5. *Identify the values of key individuals.* This includes other people, like family members, who have a stake in the final decision. Physicians, social workers, nurses, and other health care professionals may also be consulted. Again, respect is key.

6. *Identify the value conflicts, if any.* Don't ignore any disharmony or opposition. Confront it in a diplomatic manner and remind everyone whose interests are at the heart of the caregiving decision.

7. *Determine who should decide.* Who should have the final say? The primary caregiver? A spouse or other family member? Or should a health care professional call the shots?

8. *Identify the range of actions and anticipated outcomes.* Consider both negative and positive outcomes for each scenario. Which actions and outcomes can everyone live with?

9. *Decide on a course of action and carry it out.* Stay the course. Wavering on such a critical issue will only postpone the inevitable and even may make the situation more difficult for the person you're ultimately trying to help.

10. *Evaluate the results.* Don't be afraid of assessing what worked and what didn't. Eldercare situations can be adjusted and changed to fit a family's particular needs.

We often find ourselves making quick decisions—in our work, home, and personal lives. But some decisions should take time. Caring for a loved one and deciding, for example, to move that person carries with it a tremendous responsibility. In the end, you'll want to be satisfied that you carefully made the best choice. If not, you may never stop asking yourself if you did the right thing. Finding your loved one a primary care physician is a good starting point. A doctor will help a caregiver and the care recipient decide which level of care is appropriate. Plus, physicians are a good resource of local community knowledge and referrals. Remember, too, that you may need a doctor's approval or recommendation in order to qualify for certain health care services.

Before Anyone Makes a Move . . .

Before you go anywhere or move your aging relative, find out about adult day care or senior companion services. Every community is different, so you might have to dig to get the information you need. Adult day care services provide support for the physically impaired or mentally confused. However, some services cater more to one or the other rather than both. In addition to the resources listed at the end of this book, your employer might offer work-life programs especially designed for this situation.

Before you finalize your decision to move an elderly relative, make sure you can answer the following:

- How much will the move itself cost? Who will pay it?
- How much will nursing home care cost? Assisted living?
- How much time am I really willing to commit toward monitoring my relative's condition?
- Who will cover for me if I'm called out of town?
- Have I considered my relative's needs?
- Have I included my relative in the decision-making process?

If you're moving your relative to a nursing home, find out about costs and remember that Medicaid payments vary from state to state. Also, carefully think through the scenario: Will you be accessible to your loved one after the move? What happens if you're called out of town on business? Who will pick up the slack?

Principles of Caregiver Self-Advocacy:

- *Choose to take charge of your life.* Don't let your loved one's illness or disability always take center stage.
- *Honor, value, and love yourself.* You're doing a very hard job, and you deserve some quality time, just for you. Self-care isn't a luxury. It's a necessity.
- *Seek, accept, and at times demand help.* Don't be ashamed to ask for help. When people offer assistance, accept it and suggest specific things they can do.
- *Stand up and be counted.* Stand up for your rights as a caregiver and a citizen.

Source: National Family Caregivers Association, Kensington, Maryland.

A Room with a View

As you plan your retirement or weigh the options for eldercare (or do both), stay connected to the world outside. Faced with major decisions, we sometimes lose our place in life. We get so bogged down in the nitty-gritty of what needs to be done, we begin to lose sight of the big picture, the main event.

On the other hand, I know how difficult and painful major decisions can be. When my father became seriously ill with a rare and terminal form of cancer, he and my mother decided that he would spend his last days at home. What started out as his combination den/office soon turned into the room where he slept, visited with family and friends, ate some meals, and eventually died. He hated losing the battle and it tormented him to know his family was in pain. Privately, I felt he'd been cheated out of what might have been a fulfilling retirement. And while he had a bathroom close by, his computer, and a television with remote in hand, these man-made conveniences could not compare with what he beheld outdoors. Directly over where he lay is a huge panoramic window. High on the fifth floor, my father was on one side surrounded by medications and the people tending to his needs. On his right, however, was a grove of tall trees that moved with the wind and served as temporary housing for birds and butterflies. "The trees look so fragile," he used to say to my mother, "but they're really so strong in the wind."

I suppose he might have compared himself at some point to these trees, though in the end I think he might have seen his fate in the final flights of the butterflies. I'm glad he had this view on the world. I think it brought him steady pleasure, some hope along the way, and maybe even a glimpse into what would happen when he was gone.

Taking Inventory

- Give yourself plenty of time to plan.
- Think about your space requirements for now and the future.
- Educate yourself on available housing options.
- Before moving an aging relative, become well acquainted with current eldercare issues.
- As a caregiver, don't forget about your own settling-in needs.

Epilogue

A Final Word:
Empty Boxes and Other Possibilities

Frog or pearl, life hid something at the bottom of the cup.

Mary Butts, *Ashe of Rings*

Not long after we moved to our Northeastern home, a man came to our door asking if he could take some of the empty boxes we had left at the end of our driveway. He and his family were preparing to move to a neighboring town, he explained, and the boxes would come in handy.

A few days later he returned, holding a vintage photograph of my husband when he was six months old. "We found this in one of the boxes," he said. I was grateful to have the picture back but was even more appreciative of the gesture. It warmed my heart and suggested to me that we'd found a community that could easily reach out to its newcomers. From an empty box emerged a possibility, a possibility that life would be okay in this new place we called home.

Traditions and rituals are what link us to the past, keep us centered on the present, and give us hope for the future. Moving tends to interrupt the flow of these traditions. The distance between loved ones prevents a true family reunion from taking place. Friends become too scattered to adhere to the monthly dinner outing. Holidays take on a different hue when the faces you're accustomed to seeing are replaced by voices through a telephone line. Plainly speaking, things change. My sister says that the changes brought on by moving are rapid, because we no longer have wagon trains. One morning we're at one address; that afternoon we're 500 miles away.

Yet we all have a right to continue our traditions and carry out the rituals—albeit in a modified fashion—that make us who we are. It is possible to rearrange our thinking so that we can imbue our lives with comfort from the past. Our first year away from family was certainly strange and somewhat disorienting. Preparing a Thanksgiving turkey and assorted side dishes for two adults and a toddler seemed odd. Yet we carried on and learned to enjoy the company of three.

Carrying on traditions is a soothing antidote to the shifting that occurs during and after a move. Traditions affirm our commitment to the spirit of continuity. Ironically, traditions—steeped in the past—make us strong in our journey to move forward. Trying to replicate old traditions, however, can lead to disappointment and frustration. Instead, celebrate life in new ways. But be prepared if things don't work out exactly as you had planned. Traditions are started every day. Be creative, play a different role. You may rediscover yourself in the process.

Honor the Change

Moving is a great leveler. Barriers are broken. Clarity is achieved. We even get to know ourselves a little better. And as we examine the many changes that spill forth, we hone our ability to cope. As you sort through these changes, have patience and be mindful of the ripple effects. Trust your intuition and have courage that you will persevere. Respect this change and help it find a place that ultimately will make life better.

Do Unto Others

Once you've moved, you are in a perfect position to truly understand and empathize with those who follow in your footsteps. If you can, consider reaching out to your new neighbors. Recalling your own feelings as you settled into your new home, your efforts will resonate with a genuine quality that will not go unnoticed or unappreciated. Author and columnist Jann Mitchell offers these suggestions for reaching out to your new neighbors:

- Offer to help move things if you see them struggling.
- Have a pizza delivered to their home the day they move in. You supply the beverage.
- Offer to take a few photographs of them directing the movers or posing on their new porch.
- Take over a plate of cookies—store-bought megachip if you don't have time to bake.
- Provide them a new map of the city.
- Get informational brochures from the chamber of commerce, visitors' center, realty offices, or your apartment manager and put them in your neighbor's mailbox.
- Write down phone numbers of your doctors, dentist, day care center or sitter, and hairdresser, and share them.
- Offer to share your newspaper until your neighbors start their subscription.
- Let them know about garbage and recycling pickups.
- Be host for an informal neighborhood get-together so they can meet people.
- Bring them fresh batteries for the smoke alarms.
- Assemble a little care basket with first-night goodies: soap, toothpaste, toilet paper, and perhaps instant coffee, rolls, and fruit for breakfast.
- Have your children show their children the school and park.

- Invite them to call on you if they have any questions, need help, or feel lonely.
- Mark on a map the locations of the closest grocery store, barbershop, car wash, movie theater, library, etc.
- Take over a welcome treat for their pet, along with the business card of your favorite veterinarian.
- Invite them to let you know if your TV, music, kids, or dogs are ever too loud.
- Offer to baby-sit while they run errands.
- Be sensitive to their need for privacy; don't overwhelm them.

Home Is Where You Least Expect It

No matter how hard we work to recreate our dwellings, we can never predict the exact moment when that place will begin to feel like home. The familiar scent of dough rising in the oven. Unearthing a photograph that got lost and shuffled during the transition. Welcoming your first out-of-town guest. It might even occur during a mundane moment when you're washing dishes and suddenly spy a cardinal outside your kitchen window.

We all want a place in the world. Even when we find it, that place isn't always easy to keep. Some of us find it more quickly than others. Some of us might even revel in the quest and avoid capturing that place altogether. Regardless of how you define home or your place, remember that it often will be where you least expect it. So keep your eyes open, your ears to the ground, and your heart focused on what matters, and you will find that your place will, indeed, begin to feel like home.

Resources

Associations

American Association of Marriage and Family Therapists, 1133 15th Street, NW, Suite 300, Washington, DC 20005; 202-452-0109.

American Association of Retired Persons (AARP), 601 E Street, NW, Washington, DC 20049; 202-434-2277.

American Association of Retired Persons' Widowed Persons Service (WPS), 601 E Street NW, Washington, DC 20049; 202-434-2260, referrals and educational material are available.

Area Agencies on Aging, 1112 16th Street, NW, Suite 100, Washington, DC 20036; 202-296-8130.

National Alliance for Caregiving, 4720 Mongomery Lane, Suite 642, Bethesda, MD 20814; 301-652-7711.

National Association of Area Agencies on Aging Eldercare Locator. Offers a toll-free line providing a variety of eldercare resources, including home-health services, adult day care, legal assistance, and eldercare locator; 800-677-1116.

National Association of Professional Geriatric Care Managers, 1604 N Country Road, Tucson, AZ, 85716-3102; 520-881-8008. Offers referrals and educational material to assist older persons and their families in coping with the challenges of aging.

National Eldercare Referral System, LLC, is a fee-based referral service linking families with geriatric care managers, elder-law attorneys, and nursing homes; 800-571-1918.

National Family Caregivers Association, 9621 East Bexhill Drive, Kensington, MD 20895-3104; 800-896-3650. Offers support for family caregivers including a newsletter, networking, resource guide, and more.

SCORE Association (Service Corps of Retired Executives), a free one-on-one counseling service for America's small businesses; call 800-634-0245 for the SCORE office near you.

Books

Bennett, Steve, and Ruth Bennett. *365 TV-Free Activities You Can Do with Your Child.* Holbrook, Mass.: Bob Adams, 1991.

Bolles, Richard Nelson. *The 1998 What Color is Your Parachute?* Berkeley, Calif.: Ten Speed Press, 1998.

Boyer, Richard, and Savageau, David. *Places Rated Almanac: Your Guide to Finding the Best Places to Live In North America.* Englewood Cliffs, N.J.: Prentice-Hall, 1993.

Cohen, Donna, and Einsdorfer, Carl. *Caring for Your Aging Parents: A Planning and Action Guide.* New York: G.P. Putnam's Sons, 1993.

Edwards, Paul, and Edwards, Sarah. *Finding Your Perfect Work.* New York: G.P. Putnam's Sons, 1996.

Freundlich, Deborah. *Retirement Living Communities.* New York: Macmillan, 1995.

Marcus, Clare Cooper. *House as a Mirror of Self.* Berkeley, Calif.: Conari Press, 1995.

McIntyre, Mike. *The Kindness of Strangers: Penniless Across America.* New York: Berkley Books, 1996.

Moran, Victoria. *Shelter for the Spirit.* New York: HarperCollins, 1997.

Rosenberg, Lee, and Rosenberg, Saralee H. *50 Fabulous Places to Retire in America.* Franklin, N.J.: The Career Press, 1991.

Sumichrast, Michael, Shafer, Ronald G., and Sumichrast, Marika. *Planning Your Retirement Housing.* Glenview, Ill.: Scott, Foresman and Company, 1984.

Wong, Eva. *Feng-Shui, The Ancient Wisdom of Harmonious Living for Modern Times.* Boston: Shambhala Publications 1996.

Wydra, N. *Designing Your Happiness: A Contemporary Look at Feng Shui.* Torrance, Calif.: Heian, 1995.

The Internet

www.bhglive.com/moving is sponsored by *Better Homes and Gardens* magazine and offers tips for getting settled.

www.caregiving.com provides online support for caregivers, and includes excerpts from *Caregiving* newsletter and a forum to exchange ideas with other caregivers.

www.edusolutions.com is the site of an educational consulting service that helps transferring employees and their families select the right schools, from preschool to postgraduate studies.

www.expatexchange.com offers support for expatriates.

www.homearts.com is a lifestyle site from Hearst Publishing.

www.mapquest.com provides a map of your new neighborhood; TripQuest plots driving directions that lead right to your front door.

www.movequest.com offers helpful tips for settling into your new neighborhood.

www.relocationcentral.com is a compendium of helpful information, advice, and guidelines for simplifying a move.

www.relojournal.com is an excellent resource for relocation professionals, but has insightful information for consumers as well.

www.remodeling.hw.net is the home page of *Remodeling* magazine, offering an electronic portfolio of remodeling projects and consumer information.

www.welcomewagon.com is the official site of Welcome Wagon® International, offering information and resource links to other helpful sites.

Child Care

Child Care Aware, Child Care Action Campaign, 330 Seventh Avenue, 17th floor, New York, NY 10001, invites parents nationwide to call its toll-free number for information about finding quality child care and to be connected with their local child care resource and referral agency, 800-424-2246

Newsletters

Caregiving newsletter, a monthly publication containing all aspects of caregiving—emotional issues, hiring home health help, purchasing medical supplies; for subscription information, write Caregiving, P.O. Box 224, Park Ridge, IL 60068.

Kennedy's Career Strategist, a monthly guide to career planning success and job satisfaction. Published 12 times a year by Career Strategies, 1150 Wilmette Avenue, Wilmette, IL 60091.

Work and Family Life, a monthly newsletter that offers tips for balancing job and personal responsibilities; for subscription information write Work and Family Life, 317 Madison Avenue, Suite 517, New York, NY 10017, 800-278-2579.

Especially for Kids

Magazines

Babybug (Ages 2 months to 2 years)

Ladybug (Ages 2 years and up)

Spider (Ages 6 years and up)

Cricket (Ages 9 years and up)

Highlights for Children (Ages 2 to 12 years)

Jack and Jill (Ages 7 to 10 years)

Child Life (Ages 9 to 11 years)

Zillions (Ages 8 to 14 years)

"Let's Get a Move On!" (KIDVIDZ, 1990, $14.95). This 25-minute video is an entertaining guide for kids and parents. Issues covered include the impact of changing places, saying good-bye, and adjusting to new people. Call KIDVIDZ for a catalog at 800-840-8004.

Biale, Rachel. *We Are Moving.* Berkeley, Calif.: Tricycle Press, 1996. This book offers children an artistic outlet for expressing their feelings about a move. Whimsical line illustrations and lots of room for kids and their parents to color, paste pictures and mementos, and write about their feelings make this an appealing activity for everyone. Available at bookstores, or call Tricycle Press at 800-841-2665.

About Photographs

These selections will provide great tips and ideas for your budding camera buff:

King, Dave. *My First Photography Book.* New York: Dorling Kindersley, 1994. This how-to book provides a colorful visual introduction to taking pictures and making things with photographs. Children learn to master simple photographic techniques.

McKinnon, Elizabeth, and Bittinger, Gayle. *Play and Learn with Photos.* Everett, Wash.: Warren Publishing, 1994. This helps parents turn a natural curiosity into an opportunity for learning. Includes more than 100 educational photo activities for children.

About Moving

Here is a sampling of books that will help your child learn how to deal with moving to a new place:

Preschool to Third Grade

Aliki. *Best Friends Together Again.* New York: Greenwillow Books, 1995. When Robert's best friend Peter, who moved away, comes back to visit, various emotions surface, but mostly pleasure—which all the old friends share.

Asch, Frank. *Goodbye House*. New York: Simon and Schuster, 1986. Just before leaving with his family for the move to their new home, Little Bear says good-bye to all his favorite places in and around his old house.

Berenstain, Stan, and Berenstain, Jan. *The Berenstain Bears' Moving Day*. New York: Random House, 1981. The Bear family decides it is time to move to a larger house.

Komaiko, Leah. *Annie Bananie*. New York: Harper and Row, 1987. Sad because her best friend, Annie Bananie, is moving away, a little girl remembers all the fun they had together.

McGeorge, Constance. *Boomer's Big Day*. San Francisco: Chronicle Books, 1994. Boomer, a golden retriever, is confused on moving day, until he explores his new home and discovers his own toys and other familiar things.

Sharmat, Marjorie Weinman. *Gila Monsters Meet You at the Airport*. New York: Macmillan, 1980. A New York City boy's preconceived ideas of life in the West makes him very apprehensive about the family's move there.

Viorst, Judith. *Alexander, Who's Not (Do You Hear Me? I Mean It!) Going to Move*. New York: Antheneum Books for Young Readers, 1995. Angry Alexander refuses to move away if it means having to leave his favorite friends and special places.

Third Grade and Older

Hurwitz, Johanna. *Aldo Applesauce*. New York: Scholastic, 1979. When he and his family move to the suburbs, Aldo has difficulty finding new friends.

Lowry, Lois. *Anastasia Again!* Santa Barbara, Calif.: ABC-Clio, 1981. Twelve-year-old Anastasia is horrified at her family's decision to move from their city apartment to a house in the suburbs.

Park, Barbara. *The Kid in the Red Jacket.* New York: Knopf, 1987. When ten-year-old Howard has to move with his family to a distant state, he is forced to live on a street named Chester Pewe, adjust to a new school, and get used to being shadowed by the little girl in a nearby house.

Young Adults

Bethancourt, T. Ernesto. *New York City, Too Far from Tampa Blues.* New York: Holliday House, 1975. Newly arrived from Florida with his family, a young Spanish-American boy tells of his experiences living in Brooklyn and his friendship with an Italian boy who shares his passion for music.

Lingard, Joan. *Strangers in the House.* New York: E.P. Dutton, 1983. Fourteen-year-old Calvin's difficult adjustment to his mother's remarriage, their move to Edinburgh, and his 13-year-old stepsister are further complicated by the breakup of his father's second marriage.

Oneal, Zibby. *The Language of Goldfish.* New York: Puffin Books, 1990. Thirteen-year-old Carrie, clinging to memories of her idyllic early childhood, struggles to communicate with family and classmates.

Don't forget to check your local yellow pages under "Social Services" or "Social Service Organizations." There you'll find several resources that will provide a good start as you research what's available in your new area.

Index